How We Choose a Congress

How We Choose a Congress

by *Wayne R. Coffey*

ST. MARTIN'S PRESS · *New York*

Copyright © 1980 by Wayne R. Coffey

Manufactured in the United States of America
Library of Congress Cataloging in Publication Data

Coffey, Wayne R
  How we choose a Congress.

  SUMMARY: Explains the origins of Congress, its structure
and function, the differences between the two houses, the
committee and seniority systems, the process by which a bill
becomes a law, and how a seat in Congress is gained.
  1. United States. Congress. [1. United States. Congress]
I. Title.
JK1061.C583   328.73   79–26765
ISBN 0–312–39614–7

Acknowledgments

THE AUTHOR WISHES TO THANK political analysts Steven E. Presberg and Frederick Barall for their valuable insights and contributions.

Dedication

For Bill and Lorraine

Table of Contents

How We Choose a Congress

PART I

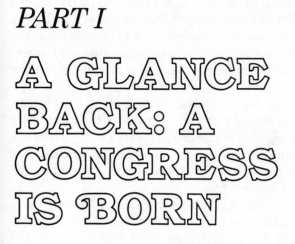

A GLANCE BACK: A CONGRESS IS BORN

THE AMERICAN REVOLUTION was a long and painful ordeal for the young United States. The bloody, bitterly fought battle against Great Britain raged for seven years, inflicting great hardship on the proud people of the thirteen colonies. Daily life was disrupted, families were separated, and, worst of all, ten thousand American patriots perished—all in the name of liberty.

Freedom exacted an enormous price from the American people, but the precious right of self-rule—which became a reality with the signing of the peace treaty on September 3, 1783—made every hardship and every casualty worthwhile. After decades of chafing under British domination, the colonists had finally broken free.

It should have been a triumphant time. It should have been a time of jubilation and optimism, of pulling together to guide the infant nation on the vital first steps toward prosperity. It should have been . . . but it wasn't. Instead, it was a time of confusion, disillusionment, and domestic strife. No sooner had the young country bravely battled out of one jungle, then it unwittingly stumbled into another.

The root of the trouble was the central government. Or, more accurately, the lack of it. The colonial experience, in which the king and Parliament of England had frequently *imposed* their will on the colonists, had taught Americans the dangers of a powerful governing body. With that in mind, they framed the Articles of Confederation. The Articles established a government which had only one branch —Congress—and which had almost no power over the thirteen states. There was no president under the Articles, nor was there a Supreme Court. Congress could not collect taxes, regulate trade between the states, enforce laws, or provide for the nation's defense.

The states were sovereign; they governed themselves and

did as they pleased. The United States was supposed to be a single nation. But actually, it was thirteen separate nations. They coined their own money, created their own trade barriers, and organized their own armies and navies. Some even made treaties and trade agreements with foreign countries.

Congress, meanwhile, became more and more impotent. Without any way to raise money to defray the national debt (which was incurred during the war years) and strengthen itself, the government came to be ignored by the states and ridiculed by other nations. "I predict the worst consequences," stated George Washington grimly, "for a half-starved limping government, always moving on crutches and tottering at every step."

A group of prominent men decided that immediate action was needed, before the "limping government" collapsed altogether. That action came in 1787. Not a moment too soon.

The Constitutional Convention

In mid-May, fifty-five state delegates journeyed to Philadelphia, Pennsylvania, to revise the Articles of Confederation. Among them were many of the leading statesmen of the time—George Washington, who later was voted president of the Convention, Alexander Hamilton, Benjamin Franklin, and James Madison, to name just a few. If ever the best minds of the young nation were needed, this was surely the time.

It was a steamy, sweltering summer in Philadelphia in 1787. But it's hard to say which was hotter, the weather or the tempers of the delegates. Confronted with a host of critical issues, debates, and disagreements, outright clashes among the delegates were inevitable. At times the disputes grew so heated that, according to Luther Martin of Maryland, the convention itself was close to collapse, "scarce held together by the strength of a hair."

The delegates were just about unanimous in their belief that the government had to be strengthened. But how much? That was the most pressing problem. One group, known as the *Federalists,* who were led by Alexander Hamilton, believed that a strong national government was essential for a smoothly functioning country. The *Anti-Federalists,* on the other hand, wanted the bulk of the power to remain with the states. "The king had a lot of power, and we all remembered what happened then," declared the Anti-Federalists. These groups ultimately became our nation's first *political parties.*

Day after day, week after week, all through the long, hot summer, the delegates doggedly debated basic questions about the nature and structure of our government. Shrouded in secrecy behind the locked doors and windows of Independence Hall, the determined statesmen realized that merely "revising" the Articles of Confederation would not be enough. They would have to start almost from scratch. And they did.

One of the first agreements was to make the government a three-part body, consisting of *legislative, executive,* and *judicial branches.* Each branch was granted certain powers, thus preventing any one branch from becoming too powerful. This is known as the system of *checks and balances.* For example, the legislative branch, or Congress, was entrusted to make *laws.* But before a law could go into effect, it had to be signed by the president. If the president chose to *veto* the proposed law, it went back to Congress, which could *override the veto* with a two-thirds majority. The judicial branch, meanwhile, was given the power to make sure that all laws were in accordance with the Constitution and did not infringe on the rights of American citizens. Thus each branch was empowered with a means to "check" the power of the other branches.

The delegates also agreed that Congress should be *bicameral,* or composed of two chambers, instead of the *unicam-*

eral structure Congress had under the Articles. But that's where consensus ended . . . and the fireworks began. The next logical issue to tackle was, Who should control Congress, the people or the states? The ensuing debate nearly shattered the Convention to pieces. It was the biggest crisis the delegates had yet confronted.

On one side were the large states, such as Virginia and Massachusetts, which advocated that both chambers of Congress be elected by the people on the basis of each state's population. Under this plan, the large states would have many more representatives, and thus more power, than their smaller counterparts. The small states, such as Delaware and Georgia, would have nothing of that.* Wary of being swallowed up by the larger states, they wanted each state to be represented equally in both chambers.

The lines were drawn, and the battle began. Caustic controversy filled the majestic hall. Patience and politeness gave way to insults and anger. Red-faced delegates made impassioned speeches, but still, the basic differences remained. Groping for a way to reduce tensions, venerable, eighty-one-year-old Ben Franklin suggested the Convention be opened with a prayer. His idea was rejected, and the bitter debate raged on. "We would sooner submit to a foreign power," railed Delaware's John Dickinson, "than to be deprived of an equality of suffrage, in both houses of the legislature, and thereby thrown under the dominion of the larger states!"

"I do not, gentlemen, trust you," declared Gunning Belford, also of Delaware. "If you possess the power . . . will you crush the smaller states?"

With each passing day, the chances of resolving the conflict appeared increasingly remote. Then, with their differ-

---

*Indeed, the smallest state of all, Rhode Island, was so incensed at the thought of strengthening the government that it refused to attend the Convention.

ences seeming impossible to overcome, Dr. William Johnson of Connecticut offered a compromise. In one branch, Johnson said, "the people ought to be represented; in the other, the states."

Reaction to the plan was hardly overwhelming. The fundamental dispute remained intact. The suspicious small states still were worried about being overpowered by the larger ones, which clung to their belief that the fairest arrangement was having directly elected congressmen according to state population. A "motley measure" was the way New York's Alexander Hamilton, who sided with the large states, appraised the proposal. Indeed, after a long, frustrating summer of scorching temperatures (remember, there were no air conditioners then!) and seething tempers, few of the delegates were in the mood to compromise. Still, a compromise was the only way out of the dilemma, and most of the delegates knew it.

A special committee studied Johnson's plan for eleven days. The committee decided that one chamber, the *House of Representatives,* would represent the states in proportion to population. The other chamber, the *Senate,* would represent the states equally. Then the committee agreed on two other provisions to appease both sides. The small states conceded the right to originate the crucial money *bills* to the House of Representatives. This pleased the large states, which, in turn, agreed to insert an article into the Constitution (which is now Article V) declaring that no state can ever be deprived of equal representation in the Senate without its consent.

Its work done, the committee submitted its plan to the entire Convention. Tension gripped the hall as each state voted on the plan. The delegates warily watched the returns, knowing if the plan was voted down, it probably would mean the end of the Convention . . . and the Union. Gradually, the states handed in their verdicts. A single vote separated them, but the plan had been approved.

Building a Congress

Thanks to the Connecticut Compromise, as Johnson's proposal came to be known, the Convention had overcome its biggest obstacle. With the foundation set, it was time to begin building the house: actually, two houses—the House of Representatives and the Senate. Board by board, the delegates hammered away until the structure of Congress was complete. Along the way, these builders had to decide a wide variety of questions about the best way to construct Congress, such as:

What should be the qualifications for the members of Congress?

The delegates decided that *representatives*—or members of the House of Representatives—must be at least twenty-five years old, a United States citizen for at least seven years, and a resident of the state in which he or she is elected.* Members of the Senate, or *senators,* must be at least thirty years old, a United States citizen for nine years, and a resident of the state in which he or she is elected.

How should members of Congress be elected?

Representatives, it was agreed, would be elected directly by the people of the districts that they serve. Senators would be elected by a vote of the legislatures of their home states. (This rather undemocratic way of choosing senators was changed by the Seventeenth Amendment to the Constitution in 1913. The *amendment* provided for the direct election of senators by the people of the states that they represent, thus making Congress a completely representative branch for the first time.)

---

*Technically, the term "congressman" refers to either a representative or a senator. But in practice, it has become synonymous with "representative." To minimize confusion here, members of the House will be referred to only as representatives. When the term congressman is used, it will encompass members of both chambers of Congress.

What should be the qualifications for the voters?

After much debate, the framers of our Constitution decided to leave voting qualifications to the individual states. Although voting laws varied from state to state, virtually all of them limited *suffrage,* or the right to vote, to white males who were well-to-do. If this does not seem democratic to you, you're right. But over the almost two hundred years since then, suffrage gradually has been expanded to include groups that had been denied the right to vote in the nation's early years.

First, the property and wealth restrictions were abolished. Then, with the passage of the Fifteenth Amendment in 1870, black males and other minority groups were awarded the right to vote. Women were extended suffrage in 1920, when the Nineteenth Amendment was passed. Finally, in 1971, the Twenty-sixth Amendment widened the right to vote to all United States citizens over eighteen years of age.

How long should the terms of office be for members of Congress?

Senators would serve a six-year term, the delegates decided. The question of the representatives' terms, however, caused quite a stir at the Convention. Some delegates believed representatives should serve a three-year term. Others vehemently objected to this, thinking that such a long stint would create too much distance between the people and their representatives. This group advocated a one-year term. "Where annual elections end," declared Samuel Adams, "tyranny begins."

So, it was time again to compromise, just as the delegates had when other divisive issues had come up. The result was a two-year term for representatives.

How large should the chambers of Congress be?

The Senate was set up to consist of two senators from each state. Thus, with thirteen states at the time, the first Senate had twenty-six members. The House, the delegates agreed, would consist of sixty-five representatives, who would be parceled out, or *apportioned,* to each state on the basis of population. The more heavily populated states would be given more representatives, the less-populated states fewer representatives. The state-by-state breakdown of representatives in the first House was like this:

State	Number of Representatives
Virginia	10
Massachusetts	8
Pennsylvania	8
New York	6
Maryland	6
Connecticut	5
North Carolina	5
South Carolina	5
New Jersey	4
Georgia	3
New Hampshire	3
Delaware	1
Rhode Island	1
Total	65

To insure equal representation, the delegates asserted that each representative would serve thirty thousand people, and that each state, no matter how small, would have at least one representative. But what about shifts in population? What if one region experiences a tremendous growth in population and another experiences a tremendous loss?

The shrewd statesmen allowed for this possibility. They decreed that a census would be taken every ten years, and that changes in population would be reflected in the composition of the House. Thus, if a particular state suffered a decline in population, it would stand to lose one or more of its seats in the House of Representatives.

It was also decided that the legislatures of each state would be responsible for drawing the boundaries of the congressional *districts* in its state.

Originally, representatives did not serve precise, well-defined *congressional districts*. But gradually, that became the accepted practice, and in 1842, a law was passed that gave the legislatures of each state the responsibility for drawing the boundaries of the congressional districts in its state. This responsibility is known as *reapportionment*. As we will see later, reapportionment can sometimes play an extremely important part in the election of our representatives.

Powers of Congress

For the builders of our nation, supplying the answers to the foregoing questions was a task of great importance. After all, without these stabilizing nuts and bolts, Congress would have been a flimsy structure that could not have lived through the trying times and constant change of our country's childhood.

Still, the most critical question of all for the busy delegates of the Constitutional Convention was, What should be the powers of Congress?

At first, the delegates considered granting Congress the power "to legislate in all cases for the general interests of the union." But what were "the general interests of the union?" What if the members of Congress disagreed about what they were? The wording of this initial proposal was too vague. So in its place, the delegates adopted Article I of the Constitution, which says, "All legislative powers herein granted shall be vested in a Congress of the United States. . . ." Then, in Section 8 of the

same Article, the delegates detailed eighteen specific areas
of those legislative powers.* Congress was given the power
to:

- levy and collect taxes
- borrow money on the credit of the United States
- regulate trade between the states and also between the
  United States and other countries
- coin money
- establish post offices
- develop a court system (other than the Supreme Court,
  which was established in another part of the Constitution)
- declare war
- provide for the nation's defense by raising and supporting an army and navy.

To make sure that the powers of Congress were distributed equally between the two branches of Congress, the
delegates granted certain powers to each. The House, for
example, was given the exclusive right to initiate all money
bills; but the Senate retained the right to vote on the money
bills (just as on all other bills) and to reject them if its
members saw fit. Similarly, the House and the Senate were
granted complementary powers regarding *impeachment,*
which is the formal filing of charges against the president.
While only the House can impeach the president, only the
Senate can try him on those charges to determine if he is
guilty or innocent.**

---

*For the complete text of Article I, Section 8 and other key selections
of the United States Constitution, see Appendix III in the back of this
book.

**The power of impeachment is the ultimate check that Congress
has on the president. Only one president—Andrew Johnson—has been
impeached in United States history. Even then, he was not convicted,
since the Senate found him innocent by a single vote. More recently,
Congress began impeachment proceedings against former President

Other powers were accorded to Congress as well. The Senate, for instance, was awarded the right to approve, or ratify, a variety of presidential actions, including the signing of treaties and the nominations of ambassadors and Supreme Court judges. The House was empowered to elect the president in the event that he failed to get a majority of the votes in the *electoral college*. (Technically, the president is not elected directly by the people, as congressmen are. Rather, he is elected by *electors,* who are distributed among the states in an amount equal to the size of the states' delegations in Congress. Thus, in the early days, a state such as Virginia, which had ten representatives and two senators, had twelve electoral votes. If, when the electoral votes for all the states were counted, no presidential candidate had a majority, then the election was turned over to the House.)

Only twice in nearly two hundred years has the House had to exercise this power. The first time was in 1800, when the House voted thirty-six separate times before Thomas Jefferson won a majority of votes and became president. The 1824 election was the second occasion. In that instance, John Quincy Adams captured the presidency on the first ballot.

To Ratify? or Not to Ratify

After four wearisome months of debate, dispute, and ultimately, compromise, the Convention disbanded and the impressive fruit of all that labor—the Constitution—was taken to the states for ratification. Nine states had to ratify it before the Constitution became the law of the land. It was by no means certain that nine states would.

Reaction to the document was mixed. Some people, such as Benjamin Franklin, admitted the Constitution had some

---

Richard M. Nixon. But Mr. Nixon resigned—the first president to ever do so—before any formal charges were actually made.

flaws, but quickly added, ". . . I doubt to whether any other Convention we can obtain may be able to make a better Constitution." Others felt the flaws far overshadowed everything else, and that the document endowed the government with too much power at the expense of the people. Congress, said delegate Richard Lee scornfully, was "a mere shred or rag of representation."

On the other side were the Federalists, led by Hamilton, Madison, and John Jay, who were among the document's most ardent supporters. Leery of entrusting too much power to the masses, whom they felt could not be counted on to make rational, well-informed decisions, the Federalists were happy with the strong, three-part system they had helped conceive. There was even a group of sort of super-Federalists who thought the Constitution wasn't strong *enough!*

Almost everyone, it seemed, had one complaint or another about the Constitution. Some thought it was too democratic; many others felt it wasn't democratic enough. But the time for debate was over; it was up to the states to make the final decision. The first to ratify it was Delaware, in December, 1787. New Jersey and Georgia followed suit. Next to give the Constitution a stamp of approval were Pennsylvania, Connecticut, Maryland, and South Carolina. That made seven. After a long and hotly contested struggle, the document squeaked through Massachusetts. Then, on June 21, 1788, New Hampshire declared its approval, becoming the ninth state to do so. On that historic day, Congress—and our system of government as we know it today—officially came into being. Two large states of great importance to the young nation, New York and Virginia, joined the others shortly after, though doing so only by a whisker. Rhode Island and North Carolina made it unanimous when they finally ratified in 1789.

Following the guidelines spelled out in the Constitution, which says, "The Times, Places, and Manner of holding

Elections for Senators and Representatives, shall be prescribed in each State by the Legislature thereof . . . ," members of the first Congress gradually were voted into office.
The debut session of our lawmaking branch was set for
March 4, 1789. But it wasn't until about a month later that
each chamber reached a *quorum,* or the presence of at least
half its members. A quorum, the Constitution says, must be
reached before the chambers of Congress can conduct official business.

With the quorum achieved, the first Congress of the
United States of America set about its formidable tasks.
Officers were elected, organizational meetings were held,
and rules were adopted. All of this was a prelude to Congress's most important task of all: making laws.

Today, almost two hundred years later, Congress is doing
much the same thing. Without doubt, our Congress is far
more complex now; how could it not be? The first Congress
had only 91 members; today that number has swelled to a
whopping 435! In 1789, Congress represented just 3.2 million people; now our legislators must look out for the interests of 220 million people! Other factors also make the job
of our present-day Congress much more difficult. Just about
every day our congressmen must grapple with problems
such as the energy crisis, the arms race, international trade
agreements, social programs for our nation's under-
privileged, and scores of other critical issues. True, Congress
had to resolve important questions in the early years as
well. But in the modern world of staggering technology,
high-speed travel, and practically instantaneous communication, Congress is faced with the nearly impossible burden
of being on top of everything at the same time. It's no wonder that Congress today introduces well over 20,000 bills in
a single, two-year session. The first Congress introduced
only 268 bills.

Still, with all the dizzying flurry of changes that have
swept through our nation and Congress over the years, Con-

gress has, in some ways, remained substantially the same. It still has the same Constitutional powers. It still is the only branch allowed to make laws. And, as one statesman said over a hundred years ago, it still is "the branch of the people."

Congress, Democracy, and You

What exactly does that phrase mean, "the branch of the people"? To find out, let's examine the word *democracy*. A word of Greek origin, democracy actually is a combination of two Greek terms: *demos,* which means people, and *kratein,* which means "to rule." Putting these two roots together, we see that democracy means "people rule." And that's the kind of system of government that we have—a government in which people rule.

This does not mean, however, that people in our government make decisions directly. Direct democracy might work in a small club or organization in which there is a manageable number of people. The town meetings that were held in many American communities in colonial times is an example of direct democracy. But as the nation's population skyrocketed, the town meeting became impractical. Can you imagine what it would be like if we had a government of direct democracy today? Can you imagine the confusion that would reign if 220 million Americans converged on Washington, D.C., to voice their opinions?

Obviously, this would not work. Nothing would ever be accomplished. So, instead of a direct democracy, we have a representative democracy. This is where Congress enters the picture. Congress is the representative branch of our government—the "branch of the people." We don't elect the justices of the Supreme Court. And, as we have seen, we don't directly elect the president; we elect him indirectly, through the electoral college. Even if we did elect the president directly—as many people believe we should—can one man possibly represent the interests and needs of millions of people, from Maine to Montana, from Alaska to Alabama? There's no way. We directly elect only one branch of our government. Congress. That's why it is the branch of the people—and the cornerstone of our representative democracy.

That is also why our senators and representatives were supplied with so much power by the men who penned the Constitution. Our founding fathers, as we have noted, disagreed over many issues. But none of them really questioned that our government should be anchored on democratic principles. It would have been extremely risky to entrust one man—the president—with the power to raise taxes, regulate trade, and make laws. Before long, we might have had another king on our hands! So, to safeguard the democracy, those and other powers were given to the people, through Congress. And, as a further safeguard, each of the three branches was delegated certain powers to create a system of checks and balances.

We, the American people, play a vital part in this scheme of checks and balances. This is because we possess the ultimate safeguard of our government and the most basic democratic right of all—the right to vote. It is this right that keeps our representatives and senators accountable to us. If we don't approve of their policies, if we don't think they've done a good job representing us, or if we believe someone else can do a better job, we can make our opinions known where it counts the most . . . at the voting machine.

No matter what happens, every two years our representatives must come back to the people of their districts and ask for their support at the polls. If, for whatever reason, he or she doesn't get that support, then another person goes to Washington. Likewise, our senators must pass the same electoral test every six years. If their performance does not meet with our approval, then the majority can exercise its Constitutional right and turn them out of office.

Some people today are skeptical about how well Congress actually represents us. Feeling that Congress has drifted away from the public, these people have become sort of "dropouts" of our political system. Many of them don't even take the few minutes it requires to vote; indeed, in a number of recent congressional elections, fewer than half of all eligible voters turned out at the polls. In light of this disinterest, it is not surprising that recent studies have shown that only about half of the American people even know who their congressmen are.

It is true, in one sense, that Congress is further removed from the people than ever before. Today, for example, a representative serves about 495,000, or just under a half million, *constituents;* the representatives in the first Congress served just over 30,000! Today's average senator serves roughly four million constituents.

Still, these figures do not mean that the people play less of a part in the political process. Each and every vote counts just as much as it always did. Our representatives and senators are still our personal officers in Washington, and we still have the right to vote for or against them. The final authority of who serves us is still in our hands.

We entrust our Congress with an enormous amount of power. Voting is our way to check that power, to make sure it is used in a manner we think is effective. If we forfeit our right to vote, there is no possible way that Congress can be the "grand depository of democratic principles" that George Mason, one of the delegates at the Constitutional Convention, hoped it would.

Election Day, then, is the time when democracy, in its purest form, emerges. That's when *we* decide who will serve us, who will be our personal connection in our sprawling federal government. But for our representatives and senators, Election Day is something else; it is the finish line of a grueling democratic race. It is a race that begins a long way back . . . long before we cast our votes. It is by no means easy. It requires hard training and tremendous stamina. It is studded with hurdles that every *candidate* must clear to win a place on *Capitol Hill*.

We have seen, in our look at the Constitutional Convention, how Congress was born and how and why it acquired its powers. Now let's look at how senators and representatives come to share in these powers. Let's look at that difficult race they must undergo and the formidable hurdles they must overcome. In short, let's look at how we choose a Congress.

PART II
EVERY TWO YEARS: THE RACE FOR THE HOUSE OF REPRESENTATIVES

Chapter 1

On Your Marks: The Candidates Step Forward

EVERY TWO YEARS, on the first Tuesday following the first Monday in November, all of the 435 seats in the House of Representatives are up for grabs.* Every two years, in every state from Hawaii to Maine, there are elections in all of the 435 congressional districts. Some of them may be close; some of them may be *landslides*. But all of them have one thing in common: the winner becomes a United States Representative.

Many people don't focus much attention on these candidates and races until Election Day draws near, until the campaign steps up and we begin to see the candidates almost everywhere . . . in the newspapers, on television and radio, on busy streetcorners, and at various community meetings. But for the candidates, this final flurry of activity is the home stretch in the race for the House. For them, the race probably began about a year before, when they "tossed their hats into the ring." Let's backtrack to the starting line, then, and take a close look at these hat-tossers.

Who are these candidates in the race for the House?

---

*This sentence may sound silly, but it really isn't. Why? Because the first Tuesday of November doesn't necessarily follow the first Monday. What if November 1 is a Tuesday? In that case, Election Day would be the following Tuesday—or November 8.

Where do they come from? Why do they run? The Constitution, as we have seen, does not have very specific requirements for representatives. To be eligible, a person need only be twenty-five years old, a United States citizen for seven years, and a resident of the state in which he wishes to run. Although not a law, it also is customary for candidates to live in the district they hope to represent.

Nowhere in the Constitution does it say that a representative must be of a certain race, sex, or social standing. Nor does it say that a representative must have a good education, a lot of money, or a particular job background.

Yet, in practice, the vast majority of representatives have many of the same attributes. Most are men; most are white. Most are from middle- or upper-class backgrounds, and most have been either lawyers, businessmen, or public officials. Virtually all of them have a college education.

This is not to say that other groups, such as women and blacks, are completely excluded from the House; there were fifteen blacks and sixteen women in the House in the Ninety-sixth Congress (1978–79). But it does mean that these and other groups are underrepresented in Congress. Why is this?

One reason is that for a long time only well-to-do white men had the right to vote. Blacks, American Indians, and other minority groups did not legally get the right to vote until 1870; women, not until 1920. Moreover, in reality the right to vote was withheld from various minority groups in some sections of the country until the 1960s. That's when the federal government abolished discriminatory devices such as the poll tax and literacy test, both of which were used by some state and local authorities to restrict the voting rights of poor, uneducated minority-group members. It follows that if people are denied the right to participate in government, they are not going to have much interest in it.

The factor of role models is also significant. An affluent white youngster whose father or grandfather was involved in politics will be much more likely to pursue that field than a black youngster whose family has had nothing to do with politics. Similarly, for a young girl growing up, politics, for a long time, did not seem a realistic option, since she probably knew very few, if any, women who were involved in it.

Think of it this way: If you are a girl, and there is an all-boy club in your neighborhood, would you want to join? Maybe, if you're brave (and the club's rules allow it!), you would. But more likely, you would feel out of place and not want to. Well, for a long time Congress was a sort of club, and it has taken a while for other groups to feel comfortable enough to join in.

With the progress that has been made through the civil rights and women's rights movements of the past two decades, it seems reasonable to expect these groups to play an increasing part in Congress and politics in general. Far more women and minority group members today have a heightened interest in politics.

So, in answer to our question—Who are these candidates for the House?—we can say this: They are more often than not white males of well-to-do upbringing, but they *can* be almost anyone: man or woman, rich or poor, black, white, or polka-dotted—as long as they meet the basic Constitutional requirements.

Where Do Candidates Come From?

Just as a particular class of people—affluent white men —are predominant in the House of Representatives, so, too, are certain professions. About half of our 435 representatives are lawyers. A good portion of them also have backgrounds in business, education, and some level of government. But this should not be taken to mean that a candidate for the House must have experience in one of these fields. We also have had Congressmen who were dentists, farmers, and accountants. We even have two men in the Ninety-sixth

Congress—Morris Udall of Arizona and Bill Bradley of New Jersey—who were professional basketball players!

Thus there is no direct breeding ground for representatives. It doesn't really matter if a candidate is a carpenter or a corporate president, so long as he is able to handle the hurdles we will discuss later.* However, it is a great help to a candidate if he has the type of job—such as practicing law —that enables him to take off for an extended period of time. Running for the House of Representatives, as we will see, is a full-time occupation for many months.

How Do Candidates Get to Be Candidates?

Candidates for the House can be divided into two groups: *self-starters* and *recruits*. If a candidate is a self-starter, he tosses his hat into the ring by himself. He has decided—for reasons we will look at shortly—that he wants to run for the House. He knows it is a long, hard race that demands great amounts of money, planning, and sheer energy, but he is so sure of his reasons that he wants to give it a go.

The recruit, on the other hand, is a candidate who is urged to join the race by a person or a group of persons. These people might be friends, business associates, community interest groups, or local political party leaders. Whoever they are, they have one conviction in common: they think the candidate would make a good representative. Here, too, the reasons for this belief vary. Perhaps the recruiters feel the candidate has good, new ideas about how to help the district, or perhaps they are dissatisfied with

---

*"He" is used here and elsewhere, instead of "he or she," purely for the sake of clarity, and to avoid disrupting sentences such as, "When he or she decides to run for office, he or she must go about the arduous task of mobilizing his or her resources." "Congressman," in lieu of "congressmen and women," or "congresspersons," is employed for the same reason. The author intends no slight toward the female population.

their present representative. Whatever their reasons (and again, we will touch on them soon), the recruiters have flattered the candidate just by suggesting he run. And if he does decide to take their suggestion, they give him a head start in the race because they are already behind him.

Actually, in many cases, the candidate is a little bit of both, partly a self-starter and partly a recruit. What does this mean? To find out, let's take the example of a mythical candidate for the House, Mr. Preston P. Peabody.

Peabody is a prominent businessman in his town. He is well liked, and he's active in such civic groups as the Boy Scouts and the Kiwanis Club. He also has been active in the local government, attending board meetings and serving on committees. For some time, he has privately entertained thoughts of running for the House. It is now January of an election year, and he's thinking more and more seriously of running. He doesn't want to announce his candidacy just yet though, because he wants to see what kind of support he can get in the community.

So instead of laying his cards out on the table, he merely tips his hand. He may drop a couple of hints while chatting with the local political party leaders. "We're not getting the representation we should in Congress," he might say. "I think it's time for a change."

Meanwhile, those same party leaders have been on the lookout for an attractive candidate for the House. They think Peabody is the man. They start dropping some hints of their own. "We need a new face in Congress, Preston," they might tell him. "We need a man who is well liked and highly respected, and who knows our needs and problems."

If the leaders feel that Peabody is receptive to their thinly veiled suggestions, then chances are they'll ask him outright if he wants to be a candidate. Peabody, of course, is delighted at this, having wanted to do it all along . . . provided he could count on some support. And now that he knows he has it, he's all set to begin the race toward the House.

Our candidate Peabody, then, is both a self-starter and a recruit. He wanted to run, but before he decided, he wanted to gauge his support in the community. Once convinced that the local leaders were just as interested in his candidacy as he was, then the "marriage" was sealed, and Mr. Peabody began to prepare for the race.

The Incumbent

In all but a small percentage of congressional districts, there is another—very formidable—candidate in the race. That is the *incumbent*, the person who already holds the district's seat in the House. An incumbent almost always seeks reelection, unless he has been involved in some kind of politically damaging scandal, is getting too old to keep pace with Congress's feverish schedule, or chooses to bow out for personal reasons. What's more, when he does seek reelection, he stands an excellent chance of succeeding. There are a number of reasons for this, which we will examine as we go along. Probably his greatest asset is that he already holds the office, and thus is well known in the district and probably something of a local celebrity. Plus he has been through the electoral race before; he knows how to glide over the hurdles and run the race effectively. Given these and other reasons, it's not too surprising that, in recent years, incumbents running for reelection have been successful more than 90 percent of the time.

This fact has made the House a place of increasing stability. From the turn of the century to the present, for example, the length of the average representative's stay has increased from about five and a half years to about eleven years. In addition, in recent Congresses almost half of the House members have served more than ten years; about 18 percent have served more than twenty years; and about 5 percent have served more than thirty years! Putting all these facts together, it means that the average Congress today has a turnover of only about 20 percent. Looking at it the other way, about four-fifths—or 80 percent—of the House membership stays the same every two years.

Why Candidates Run

Unless a candidate is thoroughly naïve, he knows that the race for Congress will be a long, hard, money-draining, energy-sapping affair. Why, then, do they run? There are a variety of reasons.

One of the most common is the prestige that goes with the office. There are hundreds of thousands of lawyers, businessmen, and teachers in our country, but there are only 435 representatives. This makes the House an exclusive and desirable place to earn a living.

Closely related to prestige is another reason for running —power. The president is the single most powerful person in our government, but Congress also plays a pivotal part in it.* To many candidates, the prospect of sharing in that power and being in on the decision-making of all kinds of important issues is a very strong incentive.

Other factors bear on the candidate's decision to run as well. Perhaps he has a keen interest in politics from his involvement locally and believes he can be of good service to the district as a representative. Or perhaps he has a more specific interest, such as the desire to see a particular piece of legislation passed—like an environmental measure or

---

*As compared to Congress, the president's power has increased markedly since the early days of the Union. It would require a book in itself to explain why, but most political scientists agree that it has to do with the increasing complexity and urbanization of our society, along with Congress's whopping membership. One man—the president—can respond to pressing issues and emergencies much more quickly and efficiently than 535 people can. Furthermore, as technology brought our vast nation closer together, the people began to look at the president—the only leader elected on a national basis—as the man who should assume prime responsibility for our government.

funds for a new highway—to help the district. He also might believe, quite simply, that the incumbent is not doing a good job.

Money also is frequently a consideration for the candidate. Representatives have a salary of $60,663, certainly a far cry from the six dollars a day the members of the first Congress were given. Still, as impressive as the present wage seems, the financial factor usually isn't the primary reason a candidate decides to run. Much of that money may have to be used to cover campaign debts. Also, the high cost of maintaining two residences—one in Washington and one in the home district—further cuts into the salary.

All of these reasons for running must be weighed by the candidate against an assortment of other considerations. First, and perhaps foremost, is the candidate's chances of winning. If the chances are very slim, it probably would not be worth his while. A candidate must also consider personal factors. What does his family think of his candidacy? Are they willing to endure the chaotic campaign schedule and the constant disruptions of daily life? Are they ready for the glaring public spotlight? For shuttling back and forth between Washington and home? What about the candidate's health? Can he withstand the rigors of the campaign, then life on the run if and when he gets to Washington? All of these considerations are given serious thought by the candidate. Only if he is certain of the "right" answers will he go through with the race.

On to the Hurdles

The candidate is firm in his reasons for wanting to run for the House. He consults his family, and they are behind him all the way. They all gear up for the long, hard race ahead. The candidate makes it official. The local newspaper reads:

Preston Peabody, a businessman who has long been active in community affairs, announced today his candidacy for the House of Representatives.

At a press conference at his new campaign headquarters on Main Street, Peabody declared, "I believe we need a fresh, new voice in Washington, and I think I'm the one to give it to us."

Peabody knows the race is only beginning. He knows he is barely out of the blocks. He knows in the coming months he is going to have to spend lots of time, energy, and money getting his message and ideas to the people of the district and convincing them he is the right man for the job.

Most of all, he knows it will not be easy. But he believes he can do it. He's ready for the first big hurdle.

Chapter 2

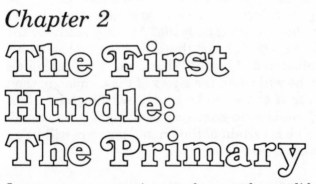

The First Hurdle: The Primary

JUST LIKE A HURDLER in a track meet, the candidate must be careful to take each obstacle one at a time. If he looks too far ahead, he might stumble. And if he stumbles, he might never be able to get back in the race.

Being first across the finish line is, of course, the new candidate's ultimate goal. But at this early point in the race, the finish line seems like miles away. He knows there is lots of backbreaking work—and difficult hurdles—ahead, before he can think about where to hold his victory party.

Accordingly, the candidate's attitude must be first things first. In order to win the election, he must be on the Election Day ballot. And in order to be on the ballot, he must win his party's *primary election.*

The candidate's first key hurdle, then, is the primary election, which is an election held for political party members of the district.* Since there are two major parties in our country—the Republican party and the Democratic party—the candidate, depending on his own party affiliation, enters either the Republican primary or the Democratic primary. In the primary, voters of the given party choose who they want to be the party's *nominee* for the regular November election.

There *are* other parties in our political system, such as the Conservative party, the Liberal party, the Labor party, and the Progressive party. These parties often field candidates for the November election. But while such minor party candidates add an interesting new dimension to the race, it is extremely rare that one of them wins the election. Also, from time to time a candidate comes along who is not affiliated with any party. Referred to as an *independent,* such a candidate gets on the November ballot by acquiring a certain number of signatures (laws vary from state to state) of the people in the district. Independents, like minor-party candidates, do not stand much of a chance of winning. There were no minor party members in either house of the Ninety-sixth Congress; there was one independent—Senator Harry Byrd of Virginia.

---

*The type of primary referred to here is a closed primary, meaning that it is closed to members of the other party. Some states, however, have an open primary, in which members of both parties can vote for any candidate, with the top two vote-getters winning a place on the ballot in November. Since the use of the open primary is so limited, it will not be incorporated into the discussion of primaries.

Gearing Up for the Primary

Before the candidate is ready to take on the all-important primary hurdle, he must get up a good head of steam. He does this by surrounding himself with a capable, hardworking staff. Led by a *campaign manager* (who will likely see more of the candidate in the coming months than the candidate's wife and family!), the staff typically consists of advisors, researchers, press agents, and general-assignment workers.

The campaign manager, usually a seasoned political veteran who knows the ins and outs of the local political scene, works closely with the candidate in mapping out a strategy for the primary. With great amounts of work to do—and little time to do it—the candidate and his campaign manager must quickly decide the best ways to build support among the party members. The first task, of course, is to make sure the candidate is highly visible and well known. To this end, the candidate may meet with local party leaders, make speaking engagements, mail out campaign literature to party members, take out advertisements in the media, and talk with community groups known to have ties with the party. In essence, these activities are the same as campaign activities for the general election in November (which we will look at in the next chapter), except that the candidate is focusing his attention on the party members, whom he needs to vault him over the primary hurdle. Once beyond the primary, the candidate will then widen his scope of campaign activities to include members of both parties.

The nature of the candidate's strategy, as well as his chances of winning the primary, depend largely on the political makeup of the district. If he is running in a *one-party district,* which is an area where one party is clearly dominant over the other, then he is likely to have much more competition in the primary itself. It isn't unusual in one-party districts for a half-dozen candidates to make a run for the nomination. There is one big consolation for the candidate in such a highly competitive situation: if he wins the primary, he is just about assured of winning the election in November.

The reason that primaries in one-party areas tend to be so hotly contested is that the dominant party generally is weak and loosely organized. Why? Because there is little incentive to have a strong, well-structured party, since the party will coast to victory in the election anyway. Thus, in a one-party district, if the candidate can survive the primary dogfight, the hardest part of the race is behind him. This is why candidates in such a region devote most of their energy and money to the primary.

As we have seen, our political system features two major parties, the Democrats and the Republicans. Because these parties are well-matched nationally, many people assume that fierce two-party competition is the basis of all elections, including those for the House. But this is not the case. In fact, in about 75 percent of the 435 congressional districts, one party is far stronger than the other. Only in about one hundred districts is there keen competition between the two. In these *two-party districts,* the parties tend to be more tightly knit and better organized; they have to be if they want to defeat the opposition party in the fall.*

The candidate who is running in a two-party district usually will have less competition in the primary, since the party's prospects for winning the general election are less certain than in one-party districts. Furthermore, the parties in two-party districts tend to try to hold down competi-

---

*There are a few one-party districts that are well organized . . . very well organized. Known as "machine" areas (because the dominant party is so efficient it resembles a machine), such districts feature party leaders who are so powerful they can pick a "machine candidate" and practically guarantee him victory in November. An example of a machine district is the Chicago area, which, in the heyday of late Mayor Richard Daley, ruled local politics with an iron hand.

tion in the primary, feeling that a bitter and divisive primary may hurt their chances in November.

No matter what type of district he is running in, however, a candidate almost always finds himself in a do-it-yourself position. There are several reasons for this. Foremost is the fact that parties and other politically active groups, such as labor and business organizations, often sit out the primary because they don't want to run the risk of supporting a candidate who doesn't wind up with the party nomination. Instead, these groups wait until the campaign, when they know who the nominee is, to furnish the candidate with support, money, and perhaps even campaign workers. In addition, public interest in the primaries is usually less intense than in the general election; thus citizens are less likely to donate either time or money in this phase of the race.*

What all this means to the candidate is that he probably will have to reach deep into his own pocket to finance his primary effort. Just how deep he will have to dig depends on how competitive the primary is. And as we know, that depends on whether the candidate is running in a one-party or two-party district.

The Incumbent: A Head Start

While most candidates for the House are going it alone in the primary, the incumbent is jumping out to a valuable head start. After all, he can count on the support of the citizens and community groups that helped elect him previously, from the moment he announces his entry into the race. Technically, the party is not supposed to support any candidate until after the primary, since the primary is held

---

*For an interesting treatment of primaries—and campaigning in general—see David Leuthold's book, *Electioneering in a Democracy* (1968).

to determine the party's nominee. But in reality, party leaders frequently help the incumbent anyway, even if it's only by advising him on strategy and speaking highly of him to friends and neighbors.

The incumbent has the additional advantage of his congressional staff, with which every congressman is furnished once he gets to Washington. The staff, which is bankrolled by the federal government, is supposed to assist the congressman in official congressional duties. Getting reelected does not fall into that category. Nevertheless, the congressional staff that does not help out in reelection bids is the exception rather than the rule.

Another big plus in the incumbent's favor is he is almost always known to more of the primary voters than any of his opponents. Unless he has received some negative publicity because of an unfavorable voting record, or worse, an image-tarnishing scandal, the candidate's greater recognition among voters is a significant advantage. What's more, the incumbent has the all-important asset of experience on his side. And he won't let the voters forget, hammering the point across in advertisements and handouts:

VOTE EXPERIENCE! VOTE CRAWFORD!
Tom Crawford knows how to work for *you* in
Washington.

Having held the office already, the incumbent also can cite his accomplishments. His message might be something like this:

Tom Crawford sponsored the drive to secure funds for our new transit system. He has worked closely with state leaders to bring 25 percent more industry to our district. He is pioneering the effort to build $3 million of new low-income housing for our elderly and underprivileged. And he's done much, much more.

Representative Tom Crawford has *done the job*. And, with your vote, he'll keep on *doing the job*.

We all need Tom Crawford in Washington.

As you can see, the incumbent can draw on a number of key advantages to get off to a head start and over the primary hurdle. He has other factors working in his favor as well, as we will see in the next chapter.

A final point to consider about the primary phase of the race toward the House is that it usually hinges on local issues. The primary candidates bear the imprint of either the Democratic or Republican party, but the involvement of the national parties just about ends there. The national party *platform,* which is its stands on important issues such as energy, inflation, and spending, does not come into play in the primary elections for the House. Much more important to the local candidate are the particular needs and concerns of the district. If there is high unemployment in the district, the candidate will discuss his ideas to bring more jobs. If there is a transportation problem, he will talk about his plans for a new bridge or highway. If there is a nearby nuclear plant that the people fear could present a health hazard, the candidate will outline his plans for more stringent safety regulations. Every district is different, and for the candidate who wants so badly to represent that district in the House, the key element in his race—from beginning to end—must be to directly address the opinions, problems, and particularities of the district's voters.

It's Primary Day

After months of hard running, our candidate Preston Peabody finally has reached his first big hurdle: the primary.* Now it's just a question of time, waiting for the results to trickle in from the district's *precincts.*

Peabody is confident. He happens to be running in a two-party district, so he does not have that much competition; only one candidate is opposing him for the party nomination. Although he respects his opponent, Peabody firmly believes he and his staff have masterminded a much sharper primary campaign.

Drawing on the financial support of an array of longtime friends, business associates, community leaders, and most of all—his own bankbook—Peabody is satisfied that he has conveyed his message effectively to party voters. He is pleased with the exposure his candidacy has received in the local media, and he's especially delighted that his painstaking efforts to focus his campaign on pressing local issues has resulted in an *endorsement* from the largest newspaper in the area.

Months of strenuous mental and physical labor—plotting strategy, making appearances, delivering speeches—have taken their toll on Preston. He is feeling a bit weary, and he wishes he could have seen more of his family. But this is nothing he didn't expect.

The polls have closed. Preston, his family, staff, and supporters are anxiously awaiting the final returns at his campaign headquarters. Finally, several hours later, the voters' verdict is in. Preston Peabody is the winner! He is officially his party's nominee for the United States House of Representatives.

Amid tumultuous cheers from his supporters, Preston thanks them for all they have done. He makes a brief speech and concludes it with words of caution: "We've got a long, difficult race ahead of us."

Peabody is overjoyed that he has cleared the first hurdle.

---

*The actual day of the primary varies from state to state, though it is usually held between April and September.

But he knows he can't afford to waste any time before preparing to leap the next one. He is in a two-party district, and he knows the biggest hurdle is in front of him. Most of all, he knows the incumbent, Thomas Crawford, already has won the other party's nomination.

"It's not going to be easy," says Peabody grimly to David Hansen, his campaign manager. "But we can do it."

Preston Peabody goes home with his family for a well-deserved night's rest. He is up early the next morning. The campaign has begun.

Chapter 3

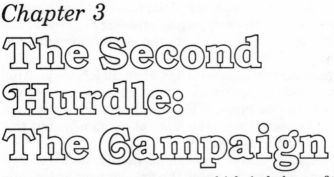

The Second Hurdle: The Campaign

TO SUCCEED AT THE WEARISOME, whirlwind phase of the race for the House known as campaigning, the candidate must accomplish a seemingly simple task: make himself known to the voters and convince a majority of them that he is the best man for the job.

It sounds easy enough. But it isn't. Overcoming the campaign hurdle requires painstaking planning, around-the-clock work, and, more often than not, lots and lots of money.

Much as in the primary, the nature and difficulty of the campaign depend on the district in which the candidate is running. If it is a one-party district, and the candidate is a member of the overpowering party, then his campaign probably will be less strenuous and less expensive. He will go through the motions, making appearances here and there, getting out to meet the people, and doing a little advertising. But since he already is past his most difficult challenge —the primary—his major concern is to make sure the people get out and vote.

The candidate running in the two-party district, however, is not so fortunate. He knows the sternest test lies ahead, and that the campaign will be an expensive, hard-fought battle between him and his chief opponent. No matter the type of district, though, and no matter how difficult a campaign fight is expected, all candidates must grapple with certain problems to overcome this crucial hurdle.*

Building a Coalition

While his campaign manager, staff, and scattered supporters may have propelled him to a primary victory, the candidate knows the campaign is a different story. He knows he now must broaden his base of power, or, in other words, build a *coalition*.

A coalition is an alliance of supporters who contribute to the candidate's campaign with endorsements, money, or campaign workers . . . and sometimes with all three. Without a solid coalition, all but the strongest one-party candidate will be doomed.

As we have noted, many interest groups, community organizations, and citizens withhold support during the primary, preferring to see who will get the party's nomination. But once the nomination is decided, they quickly line up for

---

*Again, as in the primary, the exception here is the nominee who is the candidate of a machine party. Because the machine is rich and powerful, it can make campaign life much easier for its candidate.

the campaign. The candidate's job is to lure as many of them as he can into his camp.

These supporters are drawn from a variety of sources, including the local party, civic groups, interest groups (such as labor, business, consumer, and farming), and perhaps even single-issue organizations who support or oppose causes such as abortion, the Equal Rights Amendment, or gun control.

The candidate will meet with leaders of the groups he thinks might be willing to back him; obviously, if the candidate is firmly pro-abortion, he will not arrange a meeting with an outfit that is against abortion. After outlining his reasons for running and his opinions on important campaign issues, the candidate will ask for the group's support, which, as we have seen, can take several different forms.

A group of students from a nearby university, without much money at their disposal, might help out at campaign headquarters, answering phones, mailing out literature, and talking to interested voters. On the other hand, a powerful labor union might contribute $5,000, endorse the candidate, and invite him to speak to its rank-and-file members. Whatever form the support takes, it is a valuable boost for the candidate; there is no such thing as too much money, too many endorsements, and too many workers.

As he puts together his coalition, the candidate probably will be aided by a steamroller effect; the more prominent groups and citizens he can count on his side, the easier it will be for him to line up still more. After all, everyone likes to jump on the *bandwagon* of the most impressive candidate.

Fund-Raising: Lifeline to Victory

The candidate certainly is deeply indebted to the coalition for its endorsements, workers, even its reassuring moral support. But for all candidates who are not millionaires (which means most of them), money is unquestionably the most precious resource of all.

Just like everything else, the cost of campaigning is soaring out of sight. In the 1978 congressional campaigns, for example, House and Senate candidates parted with a whopping $150 million. The *average* House candidate spent $108,000, an increase of more than 50 percent over the 1976 campaigns. One candidate, Carter Burden of New York, set a record with his $1.4 million campaign expenditures. To add insult to injury, Burden lost the election to incumbent S. William Green, who spent a *mere* $837,000.

The major force behind this skyrocketing inflation, most political experts agree, is the hefty contributions of political action committees. A recent development in campaign funding, these political action committees (PACs) are organized by special interest groups and funded by donations from group members. The money then is given to candidates whom they feel might help pass legislation beneficial to the group. For instance, a labor-based PAC might contribute to a candidate who is in favor of increasing the minimum wage, a traditional goal of labor leaders.

The impact of PACs, which legally can contribute $10,000 to a candidate, is of great concern to many members of Congress. Fearing an increasing trend toward "vote-buying," these congressmen have proposed limiting PAC contributions to House candidates to $6,000. "It is threatening to the democratic process," observed Representative Jim Wright of Texas, "if more and more of the money we receive must come from special interest groups. A seat in the House of Representatives shouldn't be ... up for sale to the highest bidder." The question of PAC contributions was debated widely—without a final decision—in the Ninety-sixth Congress.

The House also discussed the possibility of imposing a $150,000 ceiling on campaign spending in House races. No firm action was taken in this regard either. There is presently a wide assortment of federal and state campaign-spending laws, none of which has effectively controlled spending.*

No matter whether Congress passes legislation in these areas, candidates still will make fund-raising a top priority. It's a basic fact of the campaign; it takes a lot of money to run and win. So where do candidates turn?

Besides PACs, many candidates can count on a contribution from the party's national congressional campaign committee, usually on the order of $2,200. Another source the candidate can tap, especially in a district with strong party organizations, is the party's most wealthy and influential members. After extracting all he can from PACs, the party, his coalition, friends, associates—and himself—the candidate will turn to various fund-raising activities, such as luncheons, dinners, rummage sales, and auctions.

On the candidate's list of priorities, right behind how much money he gets, is when he gets it. He wants to secure as much money as he can early in the campaign. With money in the bank, he can then plan his campaign accordingly and use the funds to best advantage.

Reaching the Voters . . . and Spending the Money

The candidate is limited only by the amount of funds he has available; the ways he can spend it are virtually unlimited. As in every other phase in the race for the House, the amount he spends and how he spends it are dictated largely by the competitiveness of the race. If he is running in a

*The spiraling cost of campaign spending poses some interesting questions. Is running for Congress becoming an option open only to wealthy people? If so, doesn't this discriminate against the less privileged? Is Congress becoming a club for the rich . . . and less responsive to the needs of the poor? Congress's handling of the campaign-spending issue bears watching.

one-party district and the runaway candidate, he will not have to campaign very vigorously. But if he is locked in a tough duel in a two-party district, there will not be enough hours in the day—or enough money in the kitty—to convince him he has campaigned sufficiently.

Whatever the situation, the candidate almost always devotes a big chunk of his funds for advertising. The local newspaper is a popular forum for campaign advertising, along with radio, and, to a lesser extent, television.* By supplementing this major exposure with billboard ads, direct mailing to the voters, and an array of campaign knick-knacks—pens, posters, buttons, bumper stickers, and shopping bags—the candidate hopes to lodge firmly his name and face in the minds of the voters. The blitz is on!

As effective as this sort of recognition-building is, the candidate knows the real key to the campaign is personal contact. No matter how many times he sees and hears a candidate's name, a voter will be much more impressed with a pat on the back or a handshake. "The most important thing in campaigning is to shake hands," notes one representative. "Get out and meet the public. Let them know you are not afraid of them."**

How exactly does the candidate "get out and meet the public"? He tours factories and talks with workers. He attends neighborhood coffee klatches. He rides in a motorcade down Main Street. He attends parades and high school sports events. He shows up at supermarkets and shopping centers. He sets up a mobile office, and encourages people to stop by and say hello. He might even go door to door. In

---

*Television usually is not a major factor in House campaigns. There are two main reasons. The first is simply that the cost of TV time frequently is beyond the means of most candidates. The second is because viewing areas often go well beyond the district boundaries, the candidate feels it is not the most efficient use of funds.

**Charles L. Clapp, *The Congressman* (Garden City, N.Y.: Anchor, 1964), p. 393.

short, he is likely to make an appearance anywhere he'll get a chance to mingle with the folks he wants to represent on Capitol Hill.

Going on the *stump,* as it is called, is an exhausting way to campaign. Hour after hour, appearance after appearance, the candidate must be calm, cool, and collected, not to mention unfailingly warm and sincere. He must be ready to deliver an impromptu speech, answer questions, and deal with an occasional heckler. Most of all, he must never let up; he knows he can't afford to . . . not until that fateful Tuesday in November.

Amid all this feverish flurry of activity, the campaign manager is working just as hard behind the scenes. He is orchestrating the schedule, planning all the stops and visits. He is staying on top of the staff press aides, making sure they are feeding a constant stream of news stories to the local media. He is plotting the days ahead, ensuring the candidate makes the best use possible of the time remaining.

Furthermore, the campaign manager is responsible for keeping the candidate in command of all issues at all times. Compiling research material from the staff, direct-mail surveys, and a professional pollster he has hired, the campaign manager collects as much knowledge as he can about voters' attitudes and concerns. He passes it on to the candidate at the appropriate time. Thus, when the candidate is about to go before an environmental group, the candidate has at his fingertips all the information he needs to discuss environmental issues intelligently. Both the campaign manager and the candidate know that the worst fate for the candidate is appearing uninformed.

Endorsements

Simple statements of support from newspapers, radio and television stations, important interest groups, and prominent local, state, and national figures are of enormous value to the candidate. Getting endorsements from well-respected sources helps mold public opinion; newspapers seem to be especially effective, since they generally announce their endorsements shortly before Election Day and many voters look to the papers for guidance.

Another highly coveted endorsement for candidates is that of high-ranking national party leaders. More and more, the national parties seem to be trying to sway congressional elections by sending cabinet officers, ex-presidents, and party bigwigs to make personal endorsements in the district. Aside from casting the candidate in an important and influential light, these visits also attract extensive coverage in the media. Of course, the campaign manager will have made sure the media has been alerted about the big shot's visit to town.

Image vs. Issues

Studies have shown that, in most districts, the candidate's image has a greater impact on voters' opinions than his stands on the issues.* As a result, in all his advertising and appearances, the candidate strives to portray himself as a person who possesses the qualities that voters value the most, such as experience, intelligence, honesty, integrity, and industry.

Of course, before the candidate selects a particular quality to be the basis of his campaign theme, he must know the district and the voters.

---

*This does not hold true in those instances when one red-hot issue, such as an incumbent scandal or school bussing, dominates the campaign.

One or more of these qualities often is adopted as the campaign theme by the candidate. "Vote experience. Vote Tatum." "Let's restore honor to Washington. Let's elect Wilson." These are the kinds of slogans candidates like to employ.

Other themes candidates often hammer into the voters include youth, energy, change, and independence. After researching the district, the opponent, and the voters, the candidate and his campaign manager will choose the theme they believe is most effective. Thus, if the prevailing mood of the voters is thought to be dissatisfaction, the candidate might invoke the theme, "It's time for a change." If the opponent is an aging incumbent, youth and energy might be the attributes the challenging candidate emphasizes.

Another popular theme these days is independence, or "being an outsider." This theme, which was effective enough to play a large part in President Jimmy's Carter's election in 1976, turns inexperience into an asset. It points out that the candidate is not a part of Capitol Hill cronyism, nor a pawn of powerful special interest groups. Rather, he is an outsider, a strong-willed and independent person whose sole responsibility is to the voters.

Sometimes, in the absence of an obviously effective theme, a candidate will simply pledge to "do more." What that means may never be detailed specifically; but if the candidate is convincing, conveying the sleeves-rolled-up image of a hardworking man, it might sway the voters regardless.

All of this does not mean the candidate will never focus on particular issues; no candidate would get very far if he just ran around town screaming, "I'll do more." What it *does* mean is that, in the overall scheme, issue-taking will take a backseat to the chosen theme.

The Incumbent As Campaigner

Any candidate for the House who has ever tried to beat an incumbent over the campaign hurdle will attest that it is not an easy task. With an arsenal of weapons at his disposal, the incumbent often bursts over the hurdle without much trouble, while his opponent is left scratching and clawing. Let's examine the campaign assets that can make the incumbent so hard to unseat.

The first point to remember is that the incumbent's campaign is not limited to the months between the primary and the election. Representatives campaign constantly, in one way or another, from the moment they take office. As one House member noted, "You should say perennial election rather than biennial. It is with us every day."

Indeed, an old House adage says, "Elections are won in the off-year." Why is this? In the off-year, for one thing, the representative does not have to share the spotlight with an opponent, since there is no opponent. Without the pressure of the campaign, the representative can return home to the district and mingle leisurely with the people. He can go to dinners, attend meetings, and make low-key speeches, all without having to worry about responding to an opponent or defending his record. "You can slip up on the blind side of people during an off-year," observed one representative in Charles Clapp's book, *The Congressman,* "and get in much more effective campaigning than you can when you are in the actual campaign."

What's more, the incumbent has the advantage of running errands for his constituents. If a senior citizen back home is worried about a late Social Security check, the representative's office can place a call and speed it on its way. If a young man from the district needs emergency leave from the armed forces, the representative often can get it for him without much problem. If a small businessman needs information on government loan programs, the representative can supply that as well. There are countless other types of favors a representative can do for his constituents. These errands take time, but most representatives are happy to do them; it is the type of thing a voter remembers when it comes time to cast the ballot.

Another big plus the incumbent has is the *franking privilege*—the congressman's right to mail literature to his constituents at government expense. Designed to improve communication between Congress and the people, the franking privilege also affords congressmen an opportunity to toot their own horns by telling us what they have accomplished lately. Furthermore, when Election Day is approaching, congressmen often use the franking privilege to poll constituents to see what is on their minds. This advantage runs two ways; it flatters people that their congressman is concerned about what they think, and it gives him valuable insights about the voters' mood, thus helping him to plan his campaign strategy.

It isn't surprising that congressmen make excellent use of the franking privilege. One estimate has calculated that in a single year, each congressman franks some 900,000 pieces of mail, at an overall expense of almost $40 million.

Because they have been through it before, incumbents also have a much easier time building a coalition and gathering funds than their opponents do. After all, the incumbent only has to re-contact the groups and individuals that helped him out the last time.

Perhaps the incumbent's biggest advantage of all is simply that he is almost always better known than the other candidate. The incumbent gets more publicity, since much of what he does is considered news. He also can point to his record and tell the voters just what he has done for them; the opponent can only tell them what he *will* do. The incumbent might attend the opening ceremonies for a bridge or hospital he helped get funds for; or he might point out how legislation he sponsored has aided local industry. And, more generally, he can launch his campaign on the theme that he has been there before, and he *knows* how to work for his constituents.

When you consider the added factor that the incumbent has a government-funded staff at his disposal (which, as we have noted, is not supposed to engage in campaign activities, but indirectly at least, virtually always does), you can begin to see why most congressmen agree that "it is much harder to get in than stay in."

The Grind Is Over

"Campaigning has been even harder than I thought it would be," says a tired Preston Peabody to his campaign manager, David Hansen, who nods in tacit agreement.

It's late, the night before the big test—and the final hurdle—Election Day. The two men, weary and haggard from four months of frenzy, are unwinding in Peabody's office at campaign headquarters. The phones have stopped ringing. The staff and volunteers have gone home. For the first time since Peabody can remember, the large room isn't bustling with activity.

Leaning back in his chair, Peabody steals a glance at the newspaper lying atop his cluttered desk. The front-page headline reads:

CRAWFORD–PEABODY RACE: TOO CLOSE TO CALL

"The time went so fast," remarks Peabody wistfully. "Somehow I feel we didn't do enough."

"You can never do enough, Preston," replies Hansen with a tight-lipped half-smile. "We've run a darn good campaign. It's up to the voters now."

Hansen is right; it has been a "darn good campaign" for Peabody. Faced with the difficult task of unseating incumbent Thomas Crawford, Peabody has had surprising success in acquiring support, raising funds, and getting publicity and endorsements. From beginning to end, it has been a well-organized, carefully planned, and well-executed campaign. It had to be, for Preston Peabody to have a chance.

Scanning the room pensively, Peabody's mind races back to the countless stops on the hectic campaign trail . . . the speech before the Main Street Merchants Association . . . the brief talk at the Boy Scout dinner . . . the handshaking tour of the big textile factory . . . the successful Saturday-morning motorcade down Main Street . . . the endless meetings with neighborhood groups . . . the shopping center appearances, the doorbell ringing, the informal streetcorner rap sessions . . . and much, much more.

Thinking of all he has done—the places he has gone, the speeches he has made, the people he has met—gives Preston Peabody a sense of satisfaction. He feels he has done a solid job of reaching the voters, of expressing his views and giving them a chance to meet and talk to him. He privately feels he has outcampaigned incumbent Crawford, whom Peabody thinks—hopes—relied a bit too much on his incumbency. Only time will tell.

"C'mon, David, let's go get some rest," says Peabody softly, breaking his campaign reverie.

The two men close up shop and walk out into the brisk November night. They bid good night to each other, and David Hansen starts to his car. Suddenly, he stops and turns.

"Preston . . ." he calls loudly in the dark stillness.

"Yes?"

"Don't forget to vote."

Preston Peabody had not forgotten.

Chapter 4

The Final Hurdle: Election Day

ELECTION DAY is finally here.

Government offices close their doors. So do banks, schools, and many factories, shops, and businesses. For youngsters, it is a welcome midweek playday. But for adults from coast to coast, it is an important day . . . a day to exercise the most basic democratic right of all . . . the right to vote. Perhaps, on the local level, they will be voting for their mayors and councilmen; on the state level, for their governors and legislators; on the national level, for senators or the president of the United States. One thing is for sure, though: in this even-numbered year, just as the Constitution calls for, they will be casting ballots for their most direct links to our federal government: their United States Representatives.

For the candidates vying for one of the 435 seats in our House of Representatives, it is a day of reckoning, the day they find out if they made it over the most important hurdle of all. It also is a day of nerve-tingling anticipation, of fretful watching and waiting as the returns trickle in. After months and months on the run, the restless candidate has few outlets for his energy. The campaigning has ended. The last speech has been made, the last hand shaken. All the candidate can do now is wait . . . and hope.

Beyond the Candidate's Control

The candidate has done all he can to bring himself victory; his fate now rests with the voters. But there are several other factors—beyond the candidate's control—that can affect how the voters vote . . . and sometimes determine who goes to Capitol Hill.

One such factor has to do with the boundaries of the congressional district. We already have noted how reapportionment, as spelled out in the Constitution, redistributes districts among the states every ten years, according to shifts in population. Thus, New York, which suffered a population decline in the 1960s, lost two seats in the House. California, on the other hand, increased in population in the same period and was rewarded with five additional seats. When reapportionment occurs, the state legislatures of the affected states are responsible for *redistricting,* or redrawing the boundaries of their congressional districts.

How can this affect elections? The controlling party of the state legislature will redistrict in a way so as to help its party pick up additional House seats. This political custom, known as the *gerrymander* (after Elbridge Gerry, a governor of Massachusetts in the early nineteenth century and one of the first to engage in this practice), works like this: Suppose a Republican-controlled state is entitled to ten seats in the House. The Republicans know where the Democratic strongholds in the state are. To ensure the maximum number of "safe" Republican House seats as possible, the state will draw the district boundaries so that the vast majority of the Democrats fall in only three districts. In these districts, the Democratic candidate might win with 80 percent of the vote. But at the same time, the remaining seven seats will swing toward the Republicans, though with a smaller majority.

Another way a party can redistrict to its advantage is by spreading the opposition party over as many districts as possible. In our hypothetical state, then, the Republicans might arrange the districts in such manner that the Democrats have a minority—though a healthy minority—in, say, seven or eight districts. Thus their party again would walk off with a nice majority of the ten seats.

The political art of gerrymandering has been under close examination by the Supreme Court in recent decades. Citing population variations in some states of more than 450 percent (which means that one district in a state had 1,000 people, while another had 4,500), the Court ruled in 1964 (*Wesberry* v. *Sanders*) that "as nearly as is practicable, one man's vote in a congressional election is to be worth as much as another's."

The Court's upholding of the "one man, one vote" concept generally has made congressional districts more uniform in population. However, for two reasons, there still is room for state legislatures to gerrymander. One is that the Court has never laid down a specific standard of equality; it has never stated that population from district to district may vary only 5 or 10 or 15 percent. The second reason is that the redistricting party is still free to draw districts with highly irregular shapes in order to serve its own cause. Thus, in a Republican state, the legislature can cram an overwhelming majority of Democrats into a grossly misshapen district, such as a long, narrow rectangle, or the Democrats can do the same to the Republicans.

Another factor that can affect the outcome of House elections is the timing of the election itself. In presidential election years, for example, when more people vote than any other time House results are sometimes swayed by the *coattail effect*.

The coattail effect is when a presidential candidate wins by such a landslide that his popularity helps House candidates of his party ride into office on his "coattails." A good example is the 1964 presidential election, when Democrat Lyndon Johnson swamped Republican Barry Goldwater, and the Republicans lost forty-eight seats in the House. In this instance, Johnson's enormous popularity enabled a host of Democratic House candidates—some of whom might otherwise have lost—to gain a seat on Capitol Hill.

It should be noted, though, that the coattail effect generally is only a decisive factor in two-party districts, where the parties are fairly well balanced. In staunch one-party areas, on the other hand, not even the coattails can usually alter the people's voting habits.

The results of House races also are affected in *midterm,* or nonpresidential, election years. In these years, the party of the president almost always loses seats in both branches of Congress. Thus, in 1978, the Republicans picked up seats over President Jimmy Carter's Democratic party. Only once in the twentieth century—1934—did the administration's party pick up seats in both congressional chambers in an off-year election.

Some political experts attribute this trend to a voter dissatisfaction with the performance of the party in the White House, which, in the eyes of the people, may have failed to make good on its campaign promises. Other experts contend that, without the fanfare, additional voters, and, on occasion, the coattails that presidential elections generate, the midterm trend is simply the natural reassertion of traditional party balance. Whatever the reasons for the tendency of the party in the White House to lose seats in the House, it is clear that *when* an election is held can sometimes determine the fate of the House candidates.

It probably sounds farfetched, but another factor that can have a bearing on House races (indeed, all races) is the weather on Election Day. Bad weather, be it in the form of wind, cold, snow, or rain, tends to hurt the party favored in the election. This works in two ways. The first is purely a case of numbers. Say a district has 1,000 voters, 600 Democrats and 400 Republicans. A wild snowstorm descends on Election Day, and 500 voters stay home—300 Democrats

and 200 Republicans. Now, the 500 voters left are made up
of 300 Democrats and 200 Republicans; the difference between the parties is down to 100 voters, as opposed to 200
before. Now, the Republicans need only 50 *crossover votes*
to negate the Democratic advantage. Their chances are
much better. The other way weather hurts the majority
party is that its voters, very confident of victory, are more
likely to stay home because they are sure their party will
win anyway.

Bad weather certainly does not have the impact of the
other electoral factors we mentioned, but it can, on occasion, help contribute to a shocking upset.

The Voters Decide

The newspaper headline predicted that the Crawford–
Peabody contest for the House of Representatives was too
close to call. As Election Day winds down, neither party is
taking anything for granted. Receiving reports from their
pollwatchers of who *has* voted, and scanning party membership lists to see who *hasn't,* harried party workers
quickly place phone calls to their members, urging them to
get out and vote. Other workers organize car pools, taking
the handicapped, the elderly, and other voters to the polls.
Still others assume baby-sitting duties while young mothers
dash out to vote. These last-ditch efforts by the parties to get
out the vote may not alter the outcome; then again, they
just might. After all the work that has been done on both
sides, there is no reason to take any chances.

The polls are closed. The voters' verdict has been made,
but nobody knows what it is yet; the results are still locked
in the voting machines at precincts throughout the district.
The Board of Election workers open the machines and tabu-
late the results. Pollwatchers from each party are on hand,

carefully watching to ensure the ballots are counted correctly. The workers call Board of Election headquarters with the final tallies.

Meanwhile, tension grips the two rival camps. In a crowded ballroom at a nearby hotel, incumbent Thomas Crawford and his family, friends, and supporters nervously mingle about, reacting with alternating delight and dismay as the whisker-close returns trickle in.

On the other side of town, at party headquarters, the mood is much the same. Challenger Preston Peabody and his huge entourage anxiously await the final verdict. The tingly feeling in the large room hinges on each and every return.

"If I had been a good candidate, we'd be whooping it up by now," jokes Peabody to a few well-wishers. He tries to lighten the load, but the ever-tightening tension refuses to lift. Time passes, and the strains of watching and waiting begin to take their toll on Preston Peabody. He paces aloofly in a far-off corner. The agonizing suspense is written all over his tense and tired face. The night seems interminable. . . .

Suddenly, a flurry of returns comes in. They show Peabody doing well in a precinct predicted to go for the incumbent. A wave of muted excitement races through the room. Quickly, more returns are reported. It's more good news for the Peabody forces; their candidate has moved into a small but solid lead. The fidgety throng seems ready to burst from anticipation.

The final precincts report. . . . The crowd edges forward, sensing the big moment. . . . A whirling whoop of joy goes up in one pocket and instantly spreads to the far reaches of the room. The place erupts. Preston Peabody has done it! The final hurdle has been cleared. The race is over.

Music starts. People dance and shout with joy. Brightly colored balloons fill the air. In a matter of moments, hours of hushed tension and cautious murmuring have given way to a rollicking carnival of happiness.

A delirious Preston Peabody is the center of the swirling excitement. Scores of people rush up to shake his hand and pat his back. He flashes a grateful smile and a wink to his right-hand man, David Hansen, then escorts his wife and two young children up to the podium with him. The noise subsides. All eyes are on Peabody.

"I thought the campaign was hard," he starts, "but it wasn't anything compared to tonight." The crowd bursts with laughter. Peabody pauses. He collects his thoughts. He wonders how in the world he can thank all the people who made this moment possible. Suddenly, a soaring sense of elation comes over him. For the first time, the full force of what has happened hits him.

For the first time, he thinks of his new title . . . Representative Preston Peabody.

PART III

EVERY SIX YEARS: THE RACE FOR THE SENATE

Chapter 5

On Your Marks: The Candidates Step Forward

OUR FOUNDING FATHERS planned the United States Senate to be quite a different place from the House of Representatives. The Senate, for one thing, represented states; the House represented people, an arrangement that resulted from the Connecticut Compromise in the Constitutional Convention. The Senate was elected by the state legislatures; the House by the people. While the House was large, consisting of sixty-five members, the Senate had only twenty-six members—two senators from each of the thirteen states. What's more, senators were given a six-year term, representatives only a two-year term.

These differences did not come about by accident. They were plotted with a definite idea in mind. As we have noted, many of the delegates at the Convention were fearful of an excess of democracy in the infant nation; they were not prepared to hand over all powers of the government to the people. Alexander Hamilton summed up this sentiment when he said, "The people are turbulent and changing; they seldom judge or determine right. . . ." Hamilton and others were somewhat suspicious of the House of Representatives, which was directly elected by the people.

To alleviate this concern, it was decided that the other branch of Congress—the Senate—would be designed differently. The Senate would, as one observer put it, "restrain the fury of democracy." Its members, serving longer terms and being elected by the state legislatures, would be several steps removed from the people. What's more, the Senate would have more stability because of its rotating election system; only one-third of the senators face election every two years.

It also was agreed to give the Senate certain powers that the House did not have. Senators were granted the rights to approve treaties, confirm presidential appointments (including Supreme Court judges), and try impeachment cases. On the other hand, the most important power given solely to the House—the right to initiate all money bills—did not really amount to much. The Senate, after all, had the right to reject *any* bill that it did not approve of.

When you consider the special powers that senators had, their comfortable six-year terms, their unique method of election, and the small, exclusive nature of their branch, it is not surprising that the early senators firmly believed their branch was superior to the House. Indeed, when it came time for the first Congress to decide on its salaries, several senators were appalled at the thought of receiving the same pay as a representative. "A member of the Senate," declared Senator Ralph Butler of South Carolina, "should not only have a handsome income, but should spend it all!" The House refused to budge on this point, however, and all congressmen were awarded six dollars per day. But the uppity attitude of the senators remained intact. To them, it was not a coincidence that, in the building which housed the first Congress—Federal Hall in New York City —the Senate resided on the second floor, while the House was on the first.* The Senate thus became known as "the upper chamber," and the House "the lower chamber," though that is not a description one would want to use in the

---

*Washington, D.C., did not become the nation's capital until 1800.

presence of a representative. To this day, representatives bristle when they hear the words "upper chamber" and "lower chamber."

Despite the Senate's sense of self-importance, it was the House that was the more powerful and more effective branch in the first two decades of the Republic. Representing a large cross-section of interests, the House consistently had lively and fruitful debates, resulting in much important legislation.

However, House domination in Congress ended rather abruptly in the 1820s. Torn by the bitterly disputed issue of slavery, the states became divided into two camps. The Senate, which represented the states in Congress, became the natural forum for the slavery debate. Desperately wanting to be well represented, the states began sending their most able leaders and spokesmen to the Senate. Furthermore, with only forty-four members at the time, the Senate was the much smaller body and as a result was the more manageable place to discuss such a divisive problem.

As the decades passed, and America headed into the modern world, other factors contributed to the Senate's importance. With the expanding bureaucracy of advisers surrounding the president, the Senate's power to confirm appointments took on added significance. Likewise, with our nation's increased involvement with foreign countries, the Senate's right to ratify treaties became another feather in its hat.

Furthermore, while the House was growing by leaps and bounds, trying to keep pace with the nation's population, the Senate remained an intimate place. Not saddled with the rules and regulations the House needed to function smoothly, the Senate was more conducive to thorough, responsible discussion. The six-year term also helped the Senate gain prominence. While their counterparts in the House were constantly concerned with reelection—and thus with running errands for constituents, keeping in touch with the

district, and engaging in nearly continuous campaigning—
senators were free to focus on the larger issues confronting
their states and the nation as a whole.

"All these things," notes Donald R. Matthews in his book,
U.S. Senators and Their World, "served as powerful attrac-
tions to able and ambitious politicians."*

A Different Cut of Candidate

With this brief historical sketch behind us, let's take a
close look at the candidates who step forward for the race
to the Senate.

As in the case of representatives, the Constitution spells
out certain requirements to be a senator. A person must be
at least thirty years old, a United States citizen for nine
years, and a resident of the state which he wants to represent.** You may notice that these specifications are more
stringent than those for the representative; this difference
is another outgrowth of the Convention delegates, desire to
make the Senate a more exclusive body.

Even so, the delegates did not go so far as to require any
other qualifications to be a senator. Age, citizenship, and
residency are the only ones. The Constitution says nothing
about race, sex, wealth, education, or political experience
requirements to serve in the Senate. Yet, just as we discovered in our study of the House, nearly all Senators fit in a
certain mold. Most are white, upper-class males with a college education, and many have studied law.

This does not mean, however, that the branches of Con-

---

*Donald R. Matthews, *U.S. Senators and Their World* (Chapel Hill:
University of North Carolina Press, 1960), p. 5.

**Even the state residency requirement does not pose much of a
problem to candidates who earnestly want to run; in recent years, Robert
Kennedy (New York) and Pierre Salinger (California) quickly established
residence in those states and then won the nominations.

gress are carbon copies of each other; there are several important differences in the makeup of the Senate. For one thing, the Senate is even more homogeneous than the House; in the Ninety-sixth Congress (1978–79), there was not one black and only one woman, Nancy Landon Kassebaum of Kansas, in the Senate.* The reason for this is directly tied to the way the Senate was constructed in the Constitutional Convention. As we saw at the outset of the chapter, the Senate was designed as a small, privileged group that would guard against the unsteadiness of the popularly elected House. It remains much the same to this day, even though senators became popularly elected themselves in 1913 with the passage of the Seventeenth Amendment. From its inception, then, the Senate's privileged and prestigious standing has tended to make it less accessible than the House for women and minority groups, both of whom are relative newcomers to politics.**

The nature of the Senate accounts for other differences between the two chambers of Congress as well. Senators usually have had more prior experience in public office than representatives. In fact, in recent years more than half the senators have served for more than ten years in various public offices before their election to Congress; about 80 percent have served for more than five years in such positions.

These stepping-stone positions include the areas of local and county government, executive administration, law enforcement, and state legislature. But the most popular paths of all to the Senate is through being a governor or a representative; it's not unusual for nearly two-thirds of the senators in a given Congress to have at some point held

---

*Senator Edward W. Brooke of Massachusetts, a black, lost his bid for reelection in 1978. Prior to that, he served in the Senate for twelve years.

**The Senate also is less accessible purely because of numbers; there are only 100 seats in the Senate, as compared to 435 in the House.

either of these positions. Also, because of this wealth of political experience, senators tend to be older than representatives. The average age of today's senator is about fifty-two, some four years more than that of the average representative.

What all this tells us is that, for many politicians, a seat in the Senate is a prime ambition. Many will work their way up, building political experience in various posts—but especially as governors and representatives—in the hope of eventually securing a place in the Senate.* Thus, while some candidates for the House enter their races with little or no political experience, this is not the case in the Senate. We will see later why this experience, and the high level of recognition that goes with it, is so important for senatorial candidates.

How Do Candidates Get to Be Candidates?

Just like candidates for the House, candidates for the Senate basically can be classified as either self-starters or recruits. That is, the candidates either toss their hats into the ring by themselves, or they are sought out by friends, associates, or their parties.

However, in discussing the race for the Senate, it is important to remember that the candidate—no matter which category he falls into—is likely to be well known and have a good deal of political experience. It is equally important to realize that senatorial elections are on a statewide basis. As a result, the candidates who do emerge generally have at least some following in most parts of the state. This is in marked contrast to the House, where a candidate need only be known in his particular district.

---

*It is interesting to note that the reverse occurs very rarely; senators virtually never give up their seats to run for the House.

In short, senatorial candidates typically are not just setting out on a career in politics, as is sometimes the case in the House. Rather, candidates who emerge for the Senate already have prospering political careers and are looking to further it with their candidacy, and ultimately, with a victory in November.

The Incumbent

The feared incumbent, whom we discussed at length in the section on the House, is every bit as much of a problem for the opposing senatorial candidate. Sometimes, a candidate is so wary of taking on an incumbent that he will wait for him to retire, wait for the state's other senatorial seat to come up, or perhaps hold off long enough so that the incumbent's advancing years can be used as a campaign weapon.

In any case, the sitting senator has all the key advantages that his House counterpart has. He is well known, experienced in the job, well versed in clearing the electoral hurdles, and has an established record to run on.

Just as in the House, an incumbent in the Senate who is popular in his state can be very difficult to unseat. If the candidate is patient, and feels the state's other senator might be easier to defeat, then he should seriously consider sitting this one out.

The Pros and Cons of Running

Before joining the race, a senatorial candidate has to consider an assortment of factors. Apart from personal considerations, such as his family and health, he must give some hard thought to his prospects in the race. What is the mood of the voters? Would he be an attractive candidate to the majority of them? Does he have a big enough following? And, perhaps foremost, would he be able to raise enough money? Even more than in House races, the candidate for the Senate, as we shall see, needs to get hold of lots and lots of cash. The stakes are higher, and so is the expense.

Having seen the variables a candidate must consider, let's look at his reasons for running. His motivations, to a great extent, are the same as those of the candidate for the House. Both are attracted by the fame, power, desire to serve his nation and constituency, and, perhaps, simply a love of the fast-paced, topsy-turvy game of politics. Prestige, too, is often a reason—particularly in the Senate. With only one hundred seats in the entire branch—less than one-fourth the number in the House—the Senate definitely carries an aura of prestige.

Another factor for some senatorial candidates is the far-off dream, the quietly harbored hope, of someday moving into the big white house at 1600 Pennsylvania Avenue. Indeed, for many presidents, the Senate has been their spring-board to the highest office in the land. Certainly not every senator has presidential, or even vice-presidential, aspirations. But almost every senator, at one time or another, entertains thoughts of those coveted offices. The possibilities are not at all remote; in the last twenty-five years, roughly two-thirds of the presidential and vice-presidential candidates at one point served in the United States Senate.

On to the Hurdles

It is November of an odd-numbered year. The next senatorial election still is a year away. But if we know anything from our look at congressional races, we know the wheels of politics never stop turning. The big, bold newspaper headline reads:

REP. YOUNG WILL RUN FOR SENATE

Citing a "pressing need for new leadership and new direction," Representative Steven R. Young declared yesterday his candidacy for the U.S. Senate seat which is up for election next fall.

Representative Young, who has served in the House for ten years, told an enthusiastic group of supporters at the state capital that he is running because he wants to give "the people of our great state a more effective voice in Washington."

Although it's only the beginning, Representative Young is encouraged by the publicity and response his announcement has generated. He believes his performance in the House over the last decade has earned him a good reputation in many regions of the state. At forty, he is a young, able, and energetic leader who is determined to take his career one giant step forward.

But he is an experienced politician; he knows he has a hard race ahead. And he knows—much better than most—that the difficult hurdles in front of him will consume just about all the time, energy, and money he can muster. He knows he will have to take his message all over the state, not just to a small district. He also knows that before long, several other well-known politicians in the state will be declaring their candidacies as well.

Most of all, Representative Young knows this will be the greatest challenge of his promising political career. He is ready for the challenge. Bring on the hurdles!

Chapter 6

The First Hurdle: The Primary

THE EXCITEMENT AND ATTENTION a candidate creates when he joins the race does not last long. While he immediately plunges into the intricate plotting of the race, most voters tend to forget about it until nine or ten months later, when the election draws near. As we have seen in our look at the House races, the public generally has little interest in the behind-the-scenes legwork of the candidates and their staff and supporters.

The candidate, however, cannot afford to give scant attention to the early phases of the race. To him, the next hurdle he faces always is the most important one. Looking too far up the track—because of overconfidence or simply poor planning—often is all a hardworking opponent needs to surge into the lead.

Tackling the hurdles one at a time, then, is the careful candidate's trademark. The first hurdle for the Senate candidate, just as it is for the House candidate, is the primary election.* He has to succeed to get on the Election Day

---

*A few states, such as Connecticut and Delaware, hold nominating conventions instead of primaries. In this system, nominees are chosen by party delegates from around the state, who meet at the convention and pick the candidate they believe is the best. Because of pressure to use the more democratic method of direct primaries, choosing Senate candidates by nominating convention seems to be on the wane. This is the most recent phase of a trend that has been going on for a long time. Many years ago, virtually all congressmen were nominated by legislative caucus, or

ballot. By far the most widely used type of primary is the closed primary, in which Republican and Democratic voters each choose their party's nominee for the November election. A candidate is not obligated to run in the Democratic or Republican primaries; he may belong to another political party—or no party at all, preferring to be an independent. However, it is highly unusual for candidates other than those from the two major parties to win the election.

Gearing Up for the Primary

Just like his fellow runner for the House, the Senate candidate must get himself a capable campaign manager, and assemble an efficient staff and organization. These are the little-noticed, but all-important people whose efforts will go a long way toward determining the candidate's success in the primary. The candidate knows he would be lost without them and their valuable contributions: advising him, keeping him informed of key issues and other candidates, drafting speeches, doing research, keeping him in the news, even by answering telephones, handing out information, and talking to party voters.

Organizing these supporters is a difficult but vital task for the candidate and his campaign manager. The Senate candidate, after all, has to reach party members all over the state; in large states, such as California, Texas, and New York, that can be some chore! It's hard enough, even in the small states. Thus, whereas the House candidate can operate out of one main headquarters and perhaps several smaller ones, the candidate for the Senate has to establish a network of supporters and offices around the entire state. If you think this would cost a lot more money, you are right;

---

a select meeting of influential party leaders. Over time, that was replaced by the more democratic nominating convention, which in turn has been discarded in almost all states in favor of direct primaries.

as we will see later, Senate candidates need a very hefty supply of dollars in order to get to the people.

Aside from the pure size of the area he must be concerned with, the Senate candidate is confronted with another key factor: the broad and diverse nature of the party voters. Although especially true in larger states, this is the case in virtually all states. Unlike the House candidate, who is usually dealing with a largely homogeneous constituency, the prospective Senator has to appeal to many different kinds of people. Even within the same party, voters in different parts of the state tend to have different attitudes. A Democrat in a rural area, for example, probably will be more conservative than a Democrat from a city. To be successful, the candidate has to alter his strategy accordingly. If he is meeting with a group of small-town party members, it won't do him any good to talk of his grand plans to revitalize the big city on the other side of the state. By the same token, he won't impress the city voters with his pledge to get funds for a new highway between Dipsville and Podunk.

The bottom line for the Senate hopeful is the same as for the House hopeful—namely, to appeal to the majority of the party voters and win the primary. But, because he has to keep an eye on an entire state and not just one district, the way a Senate candidate achieves this result is more involved, more expensive, and more difficult.

The State: One-Party or Two-Party?

Another element that enters into the primary picture is the political party structure in the state. Just as in House races, the Senate candidate who belongs to the dominant party in a one-party area can expect a great deal of primary competition. This, as we have seen, is a result of the weak party organization in such states; since the party is a shoe-in to win in November, it need not worry about organizing itself to ward off a threat from the other party. The Senate candidate running in a one-party state, though, can take some comfort in that if he clears the primary hurdle, his race to the Senate is virtually over.

However, we should note that there are far fewer one-party states than one-party districts. Whereas more than three hundred House districts are of the one-party type, only about fifteen states fall into the same category. That means that roughly three-fourths of our one hundred senators hail from at least somewhat competitive two-party states. This is a recent political development. Years ago, just about half the states had one-party structures; it was unthinkable, for example, for a Republican senator to come from the South or a Democratic senator to come from much of the Midwest. In addition to a complex array of political factors, recent changes have resulted from shifts in population toward the West and South, and the growth of cities in these areas. Probably the best example of the impact of these factors is in Mississippi, where, in 1978, voters elected the first Republican senator, Thad Cochran, in more than one hundred years!

For most Senate candidates, then, the two-party system is a fact of life. The primaries in such states may be somewhat less crowded than in one-party states, since the chances of being elected in November are not as good.* Regardless, the Senate candidate from a two-party state knows that he will have a battle on his hands right down to Election Day.

But no matter what the makeup of his state, the Senate candidate is faced with the problem of tackling the hurdles, from the primary to Election Day, on his own. This is especially true in the primary, when the political parties and

---

*We say "somewhat less crowded" because often the added prestige and attraction of a Senate seat lures candidates into the field, even in a two-party state, where a primary victory by no means guarantees election.

many interest groups withhold their support until they see who gets the nomination. Indeed, it would be a waste of money for a group to pump lots of money and energy to a candidate who does not even have a place on the ballot yet.

Similarly, it also is difficult for the candidate to find volunteers and contributors before the primary. Public interest is far lower during this phase, and, as a result, citizens are not as likely to work for or give money to a candidate. Even politically active people often wait to see who the nominees are before committing themselves to a particular candidate.

The upshot of all this is that the candidate will have to rely more heavily on his own resources, and, perhaps, those of a small group of friends and supporters, to bankroll his primary campaign. Just how much money he has to come up with depends on how stiff the competition is. If he expects a fairly easy time of it in the primary, he probably will choose to save his precious dollars for the campaign. But if the primary shapes up as a free-for-all, the candidate will likely open his checkbook, roll the dice, and pray he comes out on top.

The Incumbent

Sooner or later, whether it's in the primary or the general election, the opposition candidate will usually have to square off against the incumbent. As we have seen, this is no easy task for the challenger. In order to win, he must overcome a host of incumbent advantages, such as experience, a statewide reputation, a staff, the franking privilege, and, because he has done it before, the ability to assemble a solid coalition quickly and easily.

Just as in the House, the odds are stacked against the challenger; however, the odds are *not* quite so bad for the Senate candidate. While House incumbents are reelected more than 90 percent of the time, Senate incumbents are returned to office between 75 and 80 percent of the time.* The senatorial challenger has an uphill battle, to be sure. But the hill is not as steep as it is for the House challenger. What's more, the incumbent hill is easier to scale in the general election than in the primary. This is due in part to the increased public awareness and publicity that are generated in the campaign; the challenger, in this setting, has a much better chance of consistently reaching the voters to tell them why the incumbent should be replaced.

The Focus

Throughout his harried treks crisscrossing the state, the candidate for the Senate is keenly aware that his party voters are more concerned with what he will do for them than his views on national and international issues. Once in Washington, the senator spends a good portion of his time helping to determine national policies in the areas of energy, military spending, and foreign affairs. But when he is back in his home state, stumping for votes, the challenger and the incumbent alike know the chief question of the voter is, "What will you do for *me?*"

This attitude of the voters, called localism, tends to overshadow the role of the national political parties in the races for Congress. The major candidates are either Democrats or Republicans. But, while their party affiliations may influence the voters' decisions, the party positions on larger, national issues have little impact. The result of this, as former Senator Joseph Clark has said in his book *Congress: The Sapless Branch,* is "that our legislator tends to think of himself first as a Senator from Georgia or a Representative

*The reason Senate incumbents are not as safe as their House counterparts is a function of the increasing competition among state parties. Also, because he represents a small district, the representative has a somewhat easier time making himself attractive to the constituents.

from the Sixth Congressional District of Missouri, and only secondly as a member of a *national* legislative body."*

The senatorial candidate, thus, tailors his strategy to the concerns of the voters, in both the primary and the campaign. Instead of the Middle East and defense spending, he'll talk to the voters about farm prices, his mass transit plans, urban renewal ideas, and the ways he will bring more jobs to the state. The local focus—*that* is what will help lift the candidate over the critical hurdles.

It's Primary Day

Representative Young is optimistic. Concerned . . . but optimistic. He believes he has conducted an effective primary campaign. He believes his months on the run—tireless trips back and forth across the state, meetings with county party leaders, speeches, appearances, and interviews—have succeeded in convincing the party voters that he is a top-notch senatorial candidate.

It cost a lot of money, but then, he knew it would. He feels fortunate that he was able to tap a number of friends and a scattering of organizations for financial support. He also feels fortunate that the funds he raised helped him establish a statewide network of "Young-for-the-Senate" offices.

With the invaluable assistance of his staff, he has managed to stay on top of all the key issues, to be a well-informed candidate, and to know just what to zero in on in each region he visited. Wherever he has been, big city or backwater village, he has never stopped emphasizing the all-important local issues and concerns of those parts of the state.

He has received thorough coverage in the media, secured endorsements from several influential newspapers, and ad-

*Joseph S. Clark, *Congress: The Sapless Branch* (New York: Harpe·' & Row, 1965), p. 33.

vertised carefully in areas where his party is known to be strong.

Young believes that his opponent, a longtime member of the state legislature, simply doesn't have the same name appeal that he has in the state. His opponent certainly will carry his home district and the areas surrounding it, but Young thinks his advantage in other areas is more than enough to overcome that.

Representative Young is right. He captures his party's nomination rather handily, getting almost 60 percent of the vote. It is a stirring victory for the Young camp. He just hopes the momentum will carry over into the campaign. Young knows that will be a far stiffer test, despite the fact that he is not up against an incumbent. After serving the state for eighteen years in the Senate, the incumbent was toppled in a stunning primary upset by former presidential cabinet member James Goots.

In some ways, Young is relieved that he will not have to do battle with an incumbent. But at the same time, he knows that Goots is a well-financed candidate with a solid following in the state. He also knows that his state has no guaranteed winner; neither party has consistently dominated the other in recent years.

Above all, Representative Steven Young knows that he won't just be going through the motions in this campaign, as he did when he cruised to one runaway victory after another in the House. He knows, in this race, that the candidate with the more effective campaign will be the candidate who goes to the Senate.

Indeed, a formidable hurdle lies ahead of Steven Young. There is no time to lose. After eight hours of savoring his primary victory, he is up early, meeting with his campaign manager, and raring to go. The campaign cannot wait.

Chapter 7

The Second Hurdle: The Campaign

"THE ATMOSPHERE IS TENSE, the pace hectic, the crises almost without end, and the distances traveled reckoned in the tens of thousands of miles. Adequate sleep, regular meals, and relaxation are rare luxuries in the driving quest for power. Toward the end, exhaustion sets in. . . . Then the day arrives, and there is nothing to do but await the election returns. . . . Those who end up on the long end of the tally go to Washington as United States Senators."*

Such is the tedious, tiresome, time-consuming art of campaigning for the Senate, as described by Donald R. Matthews in his book, *U.S. Senators and Their World*. No politician ever said it was easy. Some are better at it than others, but even for the best, it is not easy. It is, however, necessary. In all but the lopsided one-party states, it is the crucial phase of the race that determines which candidate goes to Capitol Hill and which one goes looking for a job. Let's see how Senate candidates try to avoid being the latter.

Building a Coalition

The seeker of a Senate seat wastes no time after the primary in assembling an alliance of supporters—or, in a word, a coalition. Just like the House candidate, he quickly

---

*Matthews, op. cit., p. 73.

expands his base of power, since the relatively small group who guided him through the primary is simply not big enough to sustain the massive campaign effort. He accomplishes this by recruiting aid from *anywhere he can*—interest groups, state and national parties, influential citizens, community organizations, and university students. Obviously, the more popular and attractive a candidate is, the easier it is for him to enlist these supporters. If he has a good track record in his previous position, and can point to the ways he has helped the state, his coalition-building will go much more smoothly. What's more, it will get still easier as he goes along, since the candidate's prestige increases with every addition to his forces.

As we have seen, the support a candidate gets may be in the form of workers, endorsements, or money. All are valuable to the candidate, though in different ways. No candidate would want to be without an army of workers who can answer phones, talk to voters, distribute leaflets and promotional material, and handle the seemingly endless assortment of loose ends around the campaign office. Endorsements, too, are a big boost; voters are impressed when groups such as labor unions or business organizations line up behind a candidate. Other types of endorsements—from newspapers, and radio and television stations—can be even more important, since these media usually are highly respected by the people and can reach enormous numbers of them.

Still, there is little question that the most prized resource of all for a Senate candidate is money. It is what makes the campaign go. And the campaign is what gets votes.

In It Comes . . . Out It Goes

One staggering statistic will suffice to tell us just how important fund-raising is to the race for the Senate: the *average* Senate candidate, win or lose, spent $920,000 in the

1978 campaign. Remember, that's the average; many candidates from the larger states parted with more on the order of $1.5 or $2 million. These figures dwarf the mere $108,000 spent by the average House candidate. If it's true for the House hopeful that "there is no such thing as too much money," then it's that much truer for Senate hopefuls. Furthermore, studies show that about 85 percent of the 1978 Senate races were won by the bigger spenders. Clearly, if a Senate candidate wants to win, he had better raise a hefty stash of cash.

Where does it all come from, you ask? Let's see. For starters, Senate candidates can count on more support from the Congressional Campaign Committees (each party has two such committees, one for each branch), generally about $10,000, whereas most House candidates get about $2,200. That's still a far cry from $1 million. Candidates also can look to individual donors—family, friends, and wealthy party members. But, apart from his own contribution (which, of course, varies on how much he has), the principal sources of money for the candidate are the powerful interest groups and political-action committees, which, as we have noted, are fund-raising groups organized by business, trade, labor, and professional associations. In the 1978 elections, it is believed that political action committees contributed more than $35 million to candidates for Congress.

These committees naturally channel their generous contributions to candidates whom they feel will represent their interests in Congress. Thus, an oil industry PAC would be a likely donor to the campaign of a senator who will vote to remove control on oil prices. Similarly, an environmental group would be a good bet to help out a candidate who has a strong record in conservation.

This trend for candidates to receive such vast sums from interest groups worries politicians and citizens alike. If, for example, a candidate accepts a huge contribution from a group, does that mean he will always support legislation that is good for them? If he does, is that thinly veiled vote-buying? Does his need to raise huge amounts of cash tend to limit a senator's independence and make him a pawn of his contributors? As one senator remarked, "The twilight zone between huge campaign contributions and outright bribes [is] murky."

The fear of what many observers feel is vote-buying has prompted Congress to consider imposing more stringent campaign-spending laws, or perhaps make federal funds available to candidates (as is the case with presidential campaigns). This is a very complex and controversial issue; some congressmen are in favor of limiting spending, while others feel it is best to leave it as "every candidate for himself." Though the debate has yet to produce any legislation, it will continue to be discussed in coming years.

As difficult as it can be for candidates to raise adequate funds, there has not been a candidate yet who has had any trouble spending it. This is especially true of Senate candidates, who, as we know, must appeal to a large and diverse constituency across an entire state.

To reach such a broad spectrum of voters, a Senate candidate employs somewhat different approaches to campaigning than his House counterpart. While both candidates have the same ultimate goal—the votes of a majority of their constituents—the Senate hopeful must travel more, spend more, and reach more people to achieve it.*

It's not only impractical—it's impossible—for a Senate candidate to personally meet a good portion of his constituents, as a House candidate can. It would be a gross waste of

---

*Obviously this is only true in the larger states. In smaller states—such as New Hampshire and Wyoming—the senator and the representative have identical constituencies.

time for him to devote too much time to standing on street-corners and appearing at shopping centers; there are many, many streetcorners and shopping centers, even in the small states. What the Senate candidate does instead is concentrate on making speeches and appearances in places where he is likely to attract a sizable group of voters. He has to focus on being seen by as many folks as he can; thus he simply cannot have the same intimate, one-to-one rapport with as many voters as a House candidate can.

This does not mean, however, that the personal touch is not important to the Senate candidate; he, too, will spend many weeks going from town to town, shaking hands with factory workers, attending luncheons and county fairs, appearing at party rallies, and making speeches to university students, community groups, labor unions, and business conventions. But the Senate candidate must guard his time jealously. He has an enormous number of people to see and miles to cover, and he simply can't afford to stay in any one place too long.

Because he can't saturate the state the way a representative can a district, Senate candidates tend to rely much more heavily on the media. As a result, more and more candidates have been turning to a media-consulting firm to handle their campaigns. What these firms are, really, are expert political packagers. They know precisely how to get maximum media exposure for their candidate. This goes far beyond advertising, though that is an important part of their job as well. Their services include scheduling appearances for the candidate on talk shows, television and radio education programs, and continuously bombarding all forms of media with a steady stream of news of their candidate. Some media consultants go so far as to film and tape a speech, press conference, or policy statement by their candidate, and then ship it to the television and radio stations in the area. Their job is to make their candidate so important, so newsworthy, that the newspapers and television and radio stations will feel compelled to feature him in the news.

In addition, media consultants do voter research and polling for the candidate, thus ensuring that he knows who he is talking to and what they are most concerned with. Packagers also mastermind the candidate's television and radio advertising efforts. Not only do they write and produce the ad, they carefully select the time spots in which they want it shown. For example, the media consultants' research has told them that certain early-morning radio stations attract a large percentage of commuting men. They also know what sorts of ads would appeal to this segment of the population. So, on the basis of this, they run an ad that is best suited to their target audience.

If all this sounds complicated to you, you are not alone. Political campaigning—especially for senators, governors, and presidents—has become increasingly sophisticated in recent years. The use of computers for polling and research, along with the advent of media experts who specialize in keeping candidates in the forefront of the public awareness, has made campaigning much more than shaking hands and mailing flyers. This trend has not changed the reality that a candidate must get out and meet the voters to be successful. But it has added a new dimension (an expensive new dimension—media consultant firms' fees easily can run into the hundreds of thousands of dollars) to campaigning.

Polishing the Image

Whether the Senate candidate uses the latest or the oldest campaign techniques, he will work harder at projecting a positive image than exploring the fine points of issues. His image, after all, will influence the typical voter more than anything else. The increased role of television comes into play here; one well-produced sixty-second television ad can do wonders in cementing the image the candidate wants to convey to the voters.

Considering its importance in determining elections, it's not surprising that candidates and their top advisers give much thought to their choice of image. They must account for the mood of the electorate, the opponent, and the best and most believable qualities of the candidate. For instance, if a young candidate is running against an aging incumbent, chances are the challenger will base his campaign on his eagerness to work and his boundless energy. In all his appearances and advertisements, he and his image-makers will take great pains to hammer home this youthful (but not so youthful that he seems unfit for such an important job!) image. Conversely, if a somewhat older candidate is running against a much younger one, he will present an image of experience, knowledge, and quiet confidence.

There are almost limitless images a candidate can employ, for each candidate has many different assets and facets to his character. However, in making the choice as to which will be most attractive to the voters, a candidate must be certain that the image is, above all, believable. A candidate's research may indicate that the voters seem particularly attracted to independence, to a strong-willed person who isn't caught up in the sticky web of Washington politics. But if the candidate has been in the Senate twenty-five years, it would be laughable were he to try to pass himself off as an outsider. He would be much better off stressing his experience.

As we have noted, this emphasis on image rather than issues is not absolute; no candidate can completely ignore the issues, because many voters *are* interested in his views and ideas. Nevertheless, it has been proven time and again that the road to Congress is best traveled by the candidate with the most effective and attractive image.

It is important to point out, however, that issues do come into play more often in Senate races than in House races.

Because Senate campaigns attract much more attention in the media and among the voters, it's only logical that the candidates are checked for content—for their opinions, proposals, and track record—more closely than House candidates. Still, after expounding on all his thoughts on the most pressing issues, the Senate candidate won't let his audience go until he wraps it all up with a flourishing, image-polishing finale.

Coping with the Incumbent

Experience. Recognition. Exposure. The franking privilege. A government-funded staff. Familiarity with voters. Ease in coalition-building. Accomplishments in office. Favors for constituents. We know, by now, what these are: the powerful weapons of the incumbent, the weapons that enable the Senate incumbent to gain reelection roughly 80 percent of the time.

The challenging candidate knows about them too—all too well. He knows, to overcome them, he has to campaign like a madman to raise money, assemble supporters, and take his case to the voters to convince them it is time for a change. It is a difficult undertaking for the Senate candidate, though, because of the wide range of voter opinions and the two-party nature of most states, not quite as hard as it is for the House candidate.

But as hard as taking on an incumbent is, the well-financed Senate candidate who does so has a powerful, highly effective weapon he can rely on—the media. Of course, the media is available to the incumbent too. Why, then, is it so critical to the challenger? Because he is the candidate who *must* boost his recognition and reputation among the voters; because he is the one who *must* convince the voters to change their minds, and send a different senator to Washington this time; because he is the challenger, facing an uphill battle, and there's no better way to climb that hill than by reaching millions of voters with his message. Television, especially, is an immediate and unrivaled way for a candidate to increase his visibility. If he has a solid corps of media experts behind him, he can become a household word practically overnight.

Having the funds to make extensive and effective use of the media does not offset the incumbent's assortment of advantages; he has a lot of aces in his hand. But it certainly can be an enormous help to a challenger in its unique ability to whisk the candidate into the homes of millions of voters. It will cost him dearly to do it. But the candidate knew, long before he even joined the race, that clearing the hurdles to get to the Senate was an extremely costly enterprise.

The Grind Is Over

For the first time in what seems like years, Representative Steven Young is home. He is home because there are no more hands to shake, towns to visit, or speeches to make. The campaign—the grueling, exhausting campaign—is over.

He hears the clock strike two. He sorely needs some rest. But he knows it would be useless; all he'd do is toss and turn.

He cannot get the campaign off his mind. It was the most trying ordeal, mentally and physically, that he has ever gone through. Worst of all, he isn't sure that all his painstaking efforts will pay off.

The latest polls show Young and his opponent, James Goots, dead even. Experts say the next senator could be decided by a paltry twenty thousand votes—1 percent of the state's voters. Young thinks for a moment how nice it would be to run for the Senate in a one-party state . . . on that party's ticket. He has no such luck.

The only comfort Steven Young can take is that he seems to have momentum on his side. He's not entirely sure what that may do for him, but he is sure he has staged a startling comeback. Several weeks ago, Goots sported a ten-point advantage in most polls, 55 percent to 45 percent. Personally, Young never felt he was that far behind, but he didn't take any chances, waging a last-ditch media blitz that had him all over the newspapers and radio and television stations. Day after day, week after week, he held press conferences, issued policy statements, outlined his plans for tackling the state's problems, and, as a last hurrah, traveled to the state's biggest city to share a prestigious platform at a huge rally with the state's other senator and a popular former governor. Apparently, all that frenzied activity paid off. . . . But Young won't know for sure until tomorrow night.

Nerve-wracking suspense in elections is new to Steven Young. He has won his last four elections to the House going away. He likes it better that way.

But then, he knew this would be much tougher. He knew he would have to campaign not in one district, but in an entire state, and that he would have to expend an enormous amount of time and energy—and more than $1 million—reaching voters in its furthest corners. He knew very well this was the price he would have to pay for his ambition, for wanting to become one of 100 senators instead of one of 435 representatives.

Whether Steven Young's ambition is fulfilled, well, that remains to be seen. His fate and his future are now in the hands of the voters.

The clock strikes three. The polls are opening in a matter of hours. Worried, weary, and wishing it over, Steven Young trudges reluctantly upstairs to bed. As he goes, he ponders one question: "I wonder how I'll be feeling this time tomorrow?"

The answer—like his fate—is out of his hands.

Chapter 8
The Final Hurdle: Election Day

THE BIG DAY is finally here. It is the first Tuesday after the first Monday in November of an even-numbered year. All over the country, millions of people are playing their part in our democracy, choosing their elected officials. On the federal level, we *know* voters will be choosing their representatives, who are elected every two years; it's 50-50 they will be choosing a president, who is elected every four years; and it's probable they will be choosing one of their two senators, who are elected every six years.

Senate elections, remember, are staggered. This means that every two years, only about one-third of the one hundred Senate seats will be up for grabs. Two years later, another third will face election, and two years after that the last third go before the voters. In giving senators six-year terms, and rotating their elections in this manner, the authors of our Constitution sought to increase Congress's stability. They reasoned that by making the Senate a continuing body, it would help offset the confusion and turnover of the two-year terms of the House.

As we have discussed, however, the incumbent's advantages and the vast number of one-party districts have greatly reduced turnover in the House. On the other hand, the increasing number of competitive two-party states has made turnover in the Senate somewhat higher. This trend, as former Senator Joseph Clark has observed in *The Sapless*

Branch, produces the "irony that the House of Representatives, intended by the Founding Fathers to be the pre-eminent organ of the popular will, is less susceptible to changes by the voters than . . . the Senate. Many House members are thus more secure in tenure and hence less responsive to the popular will than most Senators, despite the latters' six-year terms." The upshot of this trend, then, is that even though senators only go to the voters every six years, when they do, they tend to have a more difficult time getting reelected.

What the six-year stint in office—along with the staggered elections—*does* mean for the Senate candidate, though, is that his race will receive much closer attention. After all, every two years, only thirty-three or thirty-four Senate seats are open. This small number thus commands intense interest, not only statewide, but nationwide as well.

Such close inspection, in turn, often makes Senate races more affected by single-issue politics. When they are electing only one man to serve their entire state, informed voters want to know his views on the issues of the day. Depending on the state and the particular concerns of its citizens, a Senate candidate may be asked to defend his stand on nuclear power, capital punishment, abortion, military spending, or the decontrol of oil prices. Indeed, many influential interest groups with an important stake in these issues will put the candidate on the spot. "Do you favor continued use of nuclear power?" "What's your view on bussing?"

The answers to questions like these can have a great impact on Election Day. They also can make life quite uncomfortable for the candidate, who sometimes is put in a no-win position; this is especially true in the larger states with more diverse constituents. If the candidate takes one side, he will alienate the other, and vice versa. What's more, if he is genuinely undecided about the issue, he stands a good chance of being accused of waffling or being gutless.

For example, a candidate may have a large, liberal urban

center in his state. He also may have a number of military production plants which employ thousands of workers. What does he say when someone asks him his opinion on military spending? If he says he is against further increases, he will be assailed by the plant workers, their families, and conservatives for wanting to put people out of work. On the other hand, if he says he advocates hikes in military outlays, the liberals will attack him for caring more about bombs and fighter planes than the poor and needy people of the state. If he says nothing at all, everybody will complain that he's "just another politician."

This is the sort of pointed political problem that Senate candidates frequently must deal with (as must Presidential and Gubernatorial candidates). Just how they deal with it varies from candidate to candidate, as well as from state to state. If the candidate has firm convictions, and he thinks he won't be kissing the election good-bye by taking a stand, he may come right out and declare his opinion on a controversial issue. For every person he angers with his stand, he hopes there are a couple more who either agree with him, or at least respect him for his courage.

Then again, another candidate may choose to approach the hot issue more delicately, making his feelings known in a subtle, low-key fashion. Thus, to his liberal voters, he may say, "I have consistently supported programs for minorities and other disadvantaged groups." And he may very well have. But, in front of those of a more conservative bent, he may say, "I vow I will never let our country become second to any nation in military strength." If that fails to satisfy those folks, he no doubt can point to some military measure he once supported to buttress his statement. In any case, this should not be considered lying, but rather, careful, cautious, and diplomatic campaigning. The candidate simply knows how to focus on the things the people he is speaking to want to hear. And indeed, in the thousands of pieces of legislation considered in every session of Congress, there is undoubtedly something he can point to that appeals to almost everyone.

It's accepted—and expected—by almost all knowledgeable voters that a candidate will make promises in a campaign that he will not or cannot live up to. No doubt, he will be reminded of them. If the voters believe this failure is extremely serious, then he probably will not return to Washington. Conversely, if the voters think his overall performance has been favorable, then chances are they will overlook the unfulfilled campaign pledges.

Regardless, the point to remember is that Senate candidates—much more so than House candidates—tend to be checked out closely, and that this checking can influence how they fare on the big day. It also should be noted that this doesn't alter the importance of images over issues; it simply means that, for Senate candidates, issues tend to be more important than for House candidates.

Still another side-effect of the inspection given to Senate candidates is that, for better or worse, they tend to be less influenced by the coattail effect we discussed earlier. Because they are better known than House candidates, their fates at the polls more often are determined by their individual merits—or lack of them. For example, in Democrat Lyndon Johnson's landslide of 1964, the Democrats picked up thirty-seven seats in the House, but only one in the Senate. Similarly, in Richard Nixon's Republican rout in 1972, House Republicans gained twelve seats, while in the Senate, the G.O.P. actually lost two seats.

The Voters Decide

All across the state, last-minute voters hurriedly cast their ballots. They make their choices and quickly depart. The polls close. For Steven Young and James Goots, it is now just a matter of time . . . time fraught with anxiety and suspense, time that will seem like an eternity.

Camped in hotel ballrooms at opposite ends of the state's capital, the tense troops of both candidates sweat out the returns. Watching. . . . Waiting. . . . Hoping. . . . The nighttime hours dissolve grimly into morning. In homes from the biggest city to the tiniest village, voters head to bed, abandoning hope of finding out who their next senator will be until morning.

Television commentators and their all-knowing computers have projected winners in every race but one. . . . Only Steven Young and James Goots remain in the dark.

More hours pass. Outside, the city slowly arises for a new day. Inside, suspense mounts. Nearly all of the precincts have reported. The returns are unbelievably close; Goots clings to a tiny thousand-vote lead.

A short while later, the last few precincts file their returns. The voters' verdict is in; the most fleeting of looks is all that's needed to know who won and who lost.

James Goots takes the podium before his supporters. A single word is enough to shatter the despondent silence. A dejected and exhausted runner-up gratefully thanks his loyal supporters. He knows that five more votes in each precinct was all he needed to become a United States Senator. Meanwhile. . . .

Pandemonium reigns just a couple of miles away. Music plays, people dance, and victorious madness rocks the jampacked room. "Speech . . . speech," the cry goes up over the racket.

Someone snatches the microphone. "Ladies and gentleman . . . Senator Steven Young!"

The place goes berserk. Steven Young smiles broadly. It has taken forever. It has come by a paltry three thousand votes.* But his ambition has been fulfilled.

---

*If an actual vote was this close it probably would be subject to a recount. Recounts, however, usually do not change the outcome.

PART IV

OUR CONGRESSMEN'S WORLD

Chapter 9

Welcome to Washington

FOR SEVERAL WEEKS after their moments of triumph, our imaginary new congressmen—Representative Preston Peabody and Senator Steven Young—have some precious time to unwind from their grueling, nonstop races for office. But before long, they will find themselves immersed in another sort of race . . . a ratrace.

The world of Capitol Hill is, more than anything else, unrelentingly hectic. Remember, in the harried two-year life-span of each Congress, our legislators introduce more than 20,000 bills! That's quite a bit more than the 268 bills our first Congress of 1789–90 introduced. Noted historian George B. Galloway, author of *The History of the House of Representatives,* described the congressional work load this way: "Once relatively limited in scope, small in volume, and simple in nature, it has now become almost unlimited in subject matter, enormous in volume, and complex in character."*

It's not surprising then, that to the newcomer on Capitol Hill, Congress seems both bustling and bewildering. But long before he can plow into his legislative homework, the new kid on the block must resolve a host of more basic questions: Where should I live? Should I buy a house, or rent? How do I organize my office? How can I assemble a

---

*George B. Galloway, History of the U.S. House of Representatives, 2nd Ed. (New York: Thomas Y. Crowell, 1964), p. 56.

capable staff? How do I land the committee assignment I want? What do I need to know to be a good congressman?

Considering all these perplexing questions, the formal orientation our representatives and senators receive is indeed scant. Apart from information regarding office space, supplies, salary, retirement plans, and expense allowances, the newcomer is largely left to fend for himself. Former Representative Emanuel Cellar once put it this way: "The freshman Congressman is a lost soul. . . . He doesn't know the rules and nobody bothers explaining them."

Cellar made that remark about fifty years ago. Since then, Congress has made greater efforts to acquaint its new members with the strange new world in which they find themselves. Nevertheless, the sheer size and complexity of Congress's workings—even the maze of office buildings, hallways, and meeting places—make for much confusion for the overwhelmed freshmen.

Without doubt, the best way for a freshman to get his bearings is by talking with an experienced member of his branch. An inquisitive newcomer can find out more in a one-hour chat with a Capitol Hill veteran than by reading every book on Congress ever written. With the authority of a scholar, the old hand can outline for his befuddled new colleague the rules, written and unwritten, the traditions, the lifestyle, the expectations, and the accepted practices to become an effective and well-respected member.

We should note, however, that it would not be too useful for a freshman representative to seek out an experienced senator, or vice versa. Although the two branches both share Capitol Hill and reside under the name Congress, there are marked differences in the way they conduct their business. The simple size disparity between the House and the Senate accounts for the most basic difference. With 435 members, the House has, out of necessity, organized itself into a rigid, highly structured body. Having learned through the years that nothing would ever get accomplished without such a structure, the House shows an unwavering devotion to rules and regulations. It's no wonder, then, that the House rules fill an entire library!

The Senate, on the other hand, with a membership of only one hundred, can afford to be more relaxed and informal. Its members can engage much more freely in debate, and need not be so concerned with the rules and organization so essential to the House.

Learning the Folkways

In spite of the differences in makeup and procedure of the branches, all newcomers to Congress must deal with many of the same problems in order to get into the swing of things. One of the best ways to get off on the right foot is to learn —and live by—Congress's *folkways*. Let's look at these folkways, which are nothing more than accepted standards of behavior. They are not law, and they are not among the rules of either branch. But they are firmly rooted in tradition; the freshman who chooses to disregard them will find out quickly just how deeply rooted they are.

One such folkway is *apprenticeship*. This is the idea that newcomers should know their place, pay their dues, and realize that they are not yet equipped to plunge full force into legislative battle. Nothing irks senior members more than having a well-meaning but overeager beginner try to prove himself by taking center stage before he even knows how Congress works.

Not that long ago, the dictum for freshmen was "to be seen and not heard," to be a respectful spectator while the old hands showed the way to do it. This has been modified in recent years, though. The ever-increasing demands and work loads congressmen face now make it much more possible for newcomers to share the load. Nevertheless, the pushy freshman who tries to do too much too soon stands an excellent chance of alienating his colleagues. And this, in turn, will hinder his effectiveness as a legislator.

Another folkway is to be a *workhorse*, not a *show horse*. A workhorse is a member who dedicates himself to learning the ins and outs of particular issues. By focusing intently on his homework, and burrowing into his often tedious and unglamorous committee work, the new congressman will greatly impress his fellows. A show horse, on the other hand, one who seems more interested in hunting for headlines and playing to the grandstand, quickly will arouse antagonism. Before it gets too deep-seated, another member may take him aside and explain that he would be much better off concentrating on nuts and bolts before trying to build a skyscraper.

At the same time, especially in the House, the elder members know that publicity is important to the newcomers so they can show the folks back home they are doing a good job. Because of the representative's ever-present awareness that the next race is never far away, a new House member has more justification for seeking attention than his fellow freshman in the Senate.

The words of former Speaker of the House Sam Rayburn —"To get along, go along"—describe another congressional folkway. The caution here is not to make any unnecessary waves, and to cooperate with fellow members whenever possible. The age-old political art of trading votes, or *logrolling*, is part of this norm; logrolling is when politicians, each seeking to pass a piece of legislation, agree to vote for each others' interest. Or, put another way, "You scratch my back and I'll scratch yours."

The principle behind this is not for a congressman to compromise his values; if he believes strongly in an issue, he should by all means stick with it. It simply is designed to keep harmony and cooperation at a maximum, and discord at a minimum. The world of Congress is complicated enough without having members wanting to get back at each other all the time.

The folkway of courtesy is rooted in a similar goal: to keep personality conflicts out of the way of Congress's work. Conflict over issues is accepted and expected; but slinging insults and berating a colleague are not. As a result, congressmen traditionally refer to each other in such grandiose ways as: "My distinguished friend from New Mexico"; "The honorable senator from Virginia"; and "My able colleague from Iowa." When publicly debating a bill, congressmen never refer to each other by name. In fact, in the rare instances when a member is so angry he can't restrain himself, even then no name is used. "I have a minimum high regard for the gentleman," quipped former Representative John McCormack to a member who had upset him.

Such courtesy has always been a hallmark of the Senate. But in the early years in the House, you were just as likely to hear "liar" or "scoundrel" as "learned fellow" and "eminent statesman." Indeed, the House was so lively—and divided—in the first years that there were numerous instances of physical violence. Once, after a heated argument with Senator Roger Griswold of Connecticut, Senator Matthew Lyon of Vermont promptly spat a stream of tobacco juice into his foe's face. But "the spitting Lyon," as the senator became known henceforth, got his due. Several days later, in the midst of discussion, Griswold assaulted Lyon with a hickory cane. Lyon tumbled backward toward the fireplace, where he picked up a pair of cast-iron tongs. The two went at it, first dueling, then wrestling, much to the delight of the members, who were enjoying the action too much to break it up.

Such excitement—fortunately—is not a part of House life today.

A final, and more general, folkway congressmen share is a fierce loyalty to their respective chambers. Senators sometimes refer to their place of work as "the greatest deliberative body in the world." Representatives feel just as strongly about the House; as we've noted, they don't like it a bit when they hear the words "upper chamber" used to describe the Senate. But representatives and senators are united in their belief that Congress is the most important organ in our government. It is, after all, the branch of the people.

Meeting the Leaders

Having been briefed on the accepted standards of behavior, the newcomers to Capitol Hill have a much better idea of what is expected of them and how to adjust to congressional life. Now let's examine their party leaders—men who will play a very important part in their daily lives in the coming years.

First off, we should note that political parties have played an important part in Congress from the beginning. Although there is not a word in the Constitution about political parties, they came into being not long after the Convention, an outgrowth of the ongoing feud between those who wanted a strong national government and those who wanted power to reside mostly at the state and local levels. It was only natural that people with similar views on this issue would band together. That's what happened, and that's basically how our nation's first two political parties, the Federalists and the Republicans, came about.*

Political parties, in one form or another, have been with us ever since. In addition to supplying a home base for people with generally similar attitudes toward government, parties play a key role in organizing Congress and helping legislators do their jobs.

---

*After the early years, the Federalists dissolved, and eventually were replaced by the Whigs in the 1830s. Meanwhile, the Republicans underwent two name changes, first expanding it to Democratic-Republicans, and ultimately becoming the Democratic party. As the Civil War approached and the nation was divided by the slavery issue, the Whigs died out, and a new Republican party emerged. There have been changes within each party since, but the Democrats and Republicans are still with us today.

There is an established party structure in each chamber, consisting of the *majority party* and *minority party.* The majority party is simply the party with more members in the chamber, and the minority party the one with fewer. For the last twenty-five years, the Democrats have been the majority party in both houses.

At the beginning of each session of Congress (early in January of an odd-numbered year), both parties choose their officers. This is done by voting in a *caucus* or *conference,* two words that mean the same thing: a meeting of all party members of that chamber. Democrats prefer to use the term caucus, while Republicans employ conference. In any case, the Democratic caucus and Republican conference achieve the same end, namely electing each party's officers for the next two years. Let's look at the organization of the House first.

Being the majority party, the Democratic caucus is entitled to choose the chamber's most powerful leader—the *Speaker of the House.* Generally a senior member of the party who has worked his way up through the ranks, the Speaker presides over the House, and has final authority on how the branch conducts its business. In addition, he can make certain appointments, refer bills to committee, and play a large part in deciding who serves on various committees. The power of the Speaker's position depends on who is in it; but many observers believe that when a commanding figure, such as the late Sam Rayburn, mans the post, the Speaker is the second most powerful elected official, next to the president, in our government.

After electing its Speaker, the Democratic caucus chooses a *majority leader,* who is the Speaker's right-hand man and who is responsible for guiding the party's legislative goals to approval on the House *floor.*

On the other side, the Republican conference chooses its *minority leader.* Much like the majority leader, he is charged with leading the members of his party and managing the policies his party hopes to get through the House.

In addition, both the majority and minority parties choose *whips.* Supported with fifteen regional whips, each party's whip is responsible for getting party members to the floor for important votes, and serving as the link between the party's leadership and members.

In the Senate, the majority party chooses the *president pro tempore,* or the temporary president of the Senate. He is called "temporary" because the Constitution states that the vice-president shall serve as president of the Senate. In practice, this is almost never the case. Largely a figurehead position, the president pro tempore does not exercise much influence over the proceedings of the Senate.

Much more vital to the chamber's workings are the majority leader and minority leader. Chosen by their respective parties, these men are expert strategists and tacticians who employ their great knowledge of Senate activities to drum up support for their party's policies.

In their efforts, both the Senate majority leader and the Senate minority leader are aided by whips and regional whips who, like their House counterparts, are important communication cogs in the party machinery.

In both houses and both parties, these leaders serve a variety of important functions, around which all legislative activity revolves. They play a large part in determining the all-important committee assignments; as we will see, the committees of Congress are where our laws are really made. They schedule the business on the House and Senate floors. They round up party members for crucial votes, and are the hub of an informal information network that keeps their troops on top of the goings-on. On the whole, by advising, explaining, informing, and persuading their members, the party leaders are the master architects of the plans and policies the party hopes to implement.

Getting Started

The freshmen, by now, are gradually acquiring a sense of how Congress works. They are picking up on the unwritten folkways and slowly getting to know their party leaders. With this overview coming into sharper focus, the freshmen can concentrate more intently on the job they were elected to do in the first place—serve the people of their district or state. Let's look at how they get started.

Obviously, the legislator cannot do his job unless he has a place to do it. So his first step is to get an office. Allotted on the basis of *seniority,* the offices that freshmen are assigned usually are the furthest from the Capitol building. Next, the newcomer is entitled to a staff. Staff size and funding varies from member to member and chamber to chamber. Representatives from small districts receive about $200,000, while senators from large states may get three times that much. Generally, a representative has about ten staff members, and a senator about twenty. Each congressman employs a portion of his staffers in his home district or state to keep in touch with the constituents and the local issues and problems.

Every congressman will readily admit that he would be lost without his staff. Some may help him out with legislation, doing research, writing speeches, meeting with *lobbyists,* and drafting bills. Others may answer phones, type letters, and show visiting constituents around Washington. Still others may handle constituent *casework,* which entails responding to the torrent of requests, questions, and problems that come from constituents in the mail every single day.

The amount of casework a congressman handles is not to be underestimated. Most congressmen receive two hundred or more letters on a typical day, much of it from the voters back home in need of some assistance. A senior citizen may not have received her social security check and will ask her congressman to track it down. A high school student may request information for a term paper he is doing on our government. A nonprofit organization may want advice on how to obtain a federal grant for its activities. A family may be planning a trip to Washington, and they would like to be shown around. A disabled veteran may want to know the forms he needs to apply for benefits. The list is virtually endless. It's hardly surprising that a good deal more than 50 percent of the staff's time—and a good part of the congressman's time, too—is devoted to constituent casework.

While congressmen may complain about the time lost from important legislative work in running such errands, almost all of them realize just how necessary casework is. They know that, to the public, the government is a forbidding, hopelessly complex jumble of departments, bureaus, and organizations. They also know—and they cannot afford to forget—that every piece of casework can do nothing but good when it comes time for reelection. That's why congressmen keep on top of voters' requests and problems. That's why they'll see to it that just about every letter that comes in is responded to. And that's why they accept the multifaceted role of educator, adviser, investigator, problem-solver, and—not to be forgotten—lawmaker. For the congressman who chooses to focus only on the last, his stay in Washington often can be a very short one.

Nevertheless, while the congressman spends much office time on lending a hand to voters, the primary reason he was elected was to help shape the laws of our land. To serve that function, he is assigned to committees.

President Woodrow Wilson once said, ". . . Congress in committees is Congress at work." Indeed, Congress learned at the very start that the best way to handle a particular area of concern was to set up a committee. That is all a committee is: a group of members assigned to deal with a specific area of congressional business.

With the enormous and highly complex nature of Congress's work load, committees are more important today than ever before. Because they are so much smaller than Congress as a whole, they can work much more efficiently.* And because they are specialized, their members can become experts on their subject matter.** The concept behind the committee system is simple: small groups of specialists can consider bills far more effectively than a huge group of not-so-specialists. Can you imagine what it would be like if all the members of the House or Senate tried to draft a bill on intricate tax laws or advanced missile system appropriations? It would take months for the members to become knowledgeable about the field, and months more for them to agree on what should be done. It would be pure chaos! That's why Congress has committees.

There are several different types of committees. *Standing,* or permanent, committees, are the most important. It is in the standing committees and the *subcommittees*— which are even smaller, more specialized groups within a standing committee—that Congress does most of its work. There are twenty standing committees in the House and sixteen in the Senate. Within those 40 standing committees, there are some 350 subcommittees.

Another type of congressional committee is the *joint committee.* Unlike standing committees, which consist of either senators or representatives, the joint committees are made up of members of both houses. They are established when Congress feels the need for a concerted effort in a particular area. Of the nine such committees in the Ninety-sixth Con-

---

*Committee sizes vary greatly—from under ten all the way up to fifty.

**Committee membership is divided proportionately between the majority and minority parties. Thus, if there are seventy Democratic and thirty Republican senators in a Congress, a committee of ten members would consist of seven Democrats and three Republicans.

gress, the Joint Committee on Atomic Energy was the most important, being the only one with the power to *report,* or propose, its bills to the floor of both houses. The other joint committees serve as advisory panels.

Select committees are temporary bodies established to explore a special problem. Although they do not have the authority to report bills, select committees can be influential by their power to conduct detailed studies and investigations, and pass their findings on to the public, as well as other congressional committees. The best-known select committee in recent years was the Senate Select Committee on Presidential Campaign Practices, which conducted the televised Watergate hearings in 1974. Headed by Senator Sam Ervin, the committee's findings led to the start of impeachment proceedings against President Nixon, and, ultimately, his resignation.

The final type of committee is the *conference committee.* A special, temporary body, the conference committee concerns itself with only one bill. After a bill has been approved by both houses, it then goes to a conference committee for final revision. This is necessary because usually the bill has undergone changes as it passed through each house. It is the job of the conference committee to iron out the differences of the two versions, and then send it back to the floor of each house for final approval.* With its job completed, the conference committee disbands.

The Committee Assignments

The first key challenge for newcomers to Congress is to land a spot on a desirable committee.** What "desirable" is depends on the congressman and the district or state he

---

*The way the committee system works will be examined in detail in the next chapter.

**Unless otherwise stated, readers should assume the word committee means standing committee.

represents. For a representative from the Midwest, a place on the House Agriculture Committee would be ideal. For a senator from a large state with many urban centers, the Senate Committee on Labor and Human Resources would seem appropriate. Generally, congressmen like to be assigned to a committee that they are not only interested in, but also that would be of some benefit to their constituents.

Because committee assignments are so important, the wise newcomers will do everything they can to influence the various committees of party leaders that make the assignments; there are four such *committees on committees* in Congress—one for each party in each branch. While these committees must weigh a number of factors—vacancies, seniority, regional balance, and the interests of a member's constituents—it can't hurt for the freshman to make his preferences known.* Typically, he does this by talking to party leaders, senior members from his state or region, and making the strongest case possible for his assignment to the committee in which he is interested. If he's lucky, and he's made a good argument for himself, he'll get the assignment he wanted. If he's not so fortunate—and he is still around for the next Congress—he can always apply for another committee.

Two other points concerning committee assignment should be made. First, because there are more congressmen than committees and subcommittees, members are assigned to more than one.** In the House, a representative might serve on two committees and three or four subcommittees. In the Senate, where membership is much smaller, a mem-

---

*In assigning committees, party leaders try to seat members from as many different regions as possible, so as to avoid regional favoritism. They also give preference to senior members. Thus, a newcomer is out of luck if a senior member from his region seeks an assignment to the same committee.

**Subcommittee assignments are made by the committee chairman.

ber might serve on three committees and often ten subcommittees.

Second, as a general—though not binding—rule, freshmen do not get assigned to the most powerful and prestigious committees. In the House, this includes Ways and Means, Rules, and Appropriations; in the Senate, Foreign Relations, Finance, and Appropriations. Congressmen usually have to be around for a while before getting a seat on these committees. Although many congressmen make it a top priority to secure a seat on a powerful, highly visible committee, lots of others are content to stay put on the panel to which they were first assigned. The key advantage to sticking with a committee is the opportunity to build seniority; the longer a congressman serves on a committee, the better his chances of increasing his power, and, ultimately, becoming either chairman or the highest-ranking minority party member. In any case, whether a congressman decides to switch committees depends on his ambition, his interests, and where he can best serve his constituents.

Falling into the Flow . . .

After a hectic and often baffling period of adjustment, Representative Preston Peabody feels much more at home in the House. Actually, Peabody's orientation has been much smoother than it has been for most of his fellow freshmen. Thanks to the sage advice from one of his party's top leaders, who happens to hail from the district right next to his, Peabody learned a whole lot about the House in a hurry. He learned about the House folkways and gained some valuable insights on how to assemble a first-rate staff. Peabody also picked up a priceless word of caution from the old hand: "Don't ever neglect the folks back home. They put you here . . . and they can just as easily take you away."

What's more, the party leader helped Peabody get assigned to the House Public Works and Transportation Committee, which was the freshman's top choice. Through his role in this committee, Peabody hopes to help acquire funds to build a new and badly needed highway in his district. That way, when it comes time for reelection in two years, he can point to how he has served his constituents.

On the other side of the Capitol, our new senator, Steven Young, is finding his initial taste of Senate life to his liking. Although, after ten years in the House, he is at the bottom of the Senate's seniority ladder, he feels it is well worth it. For one thing, he's delighted he won't have to face reelection in two years. He likes the informality and intimacy of the smaller chamber, too, and besides, he knows it offers a greater chance for national recognition. From his newly assigned berth on the Senate Armed Services Committee, he eventually hopes to move up to the Senate Foreign Relations Committee, where he will be able to help shape our nation's foreign policy. But before he can do that, Young knows he must dedicate himself to his committee work, and earn the respect of his fellow senators. He did that in the House, and Senator Young is confident that once he gets to know his new home and colleagues, he'll be able to do it in the Senate.

Having gotten settled in their new jobs, our congressmen now can focus on their demanding day-to-day schedules. They know they are faced with a staggering work load. They know an enormous challenge awaits them and their colleagues: to make laws for a nation of 220 million people. Let's see how Congress tackles this challenge.

Chapter 10

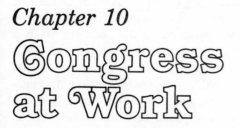

Congress at Work

THE DAY BEGINS EARLY on Capitol Hill, and it ends late. The first scattered signs of activity can be seen not long after the morning sun first glistens against the majestic marble dome of the Capitol. It may not end until long after the sun has run its daily course, shrouding the dome in darkness.

For many of our Congressmen, fourteen- to sixteen-hour days, six, sometimes seven, days a week, is not an unusual schedule. Indeed, the biggest adjustment of all for newcomers to the Hill is getting used to life on the run. Even with this maddening pace, which is maintained for the nine or more months Congress is in session each year, our congressmen cannot hope to finish all their work. That's perhaps the best measure of just how heavy their work load is. It's also a measure of the long and perilous process a bill must survive in order to become a law.

How a Bill Becomes a Law

A bill, quite simply, is a proposed law. It is introduced to Congress because a group of citizens, a special interest group, an executive agency, the president, or a member of Congress itself believes that it is worthwhile. Perhaps it is a bill to impose a tax on oil companies. Perhaps it is a bill to establish a trade agreement with a foreign country. Or perhaps it is a bill to improve mass-transit systems in big cities. These are all known as public bills; they deal with broad issues which affect many people. Another kind of bill

107

is the private bill; this pertains to an individual citizen or group of citizens. A private bill, for example, might propose compensation for a person injured in an accident with a government vehicle, or suggest that a foreign person—who otherwise might have to leave—be allowed to stay in our country. Private bills generally are passed quickly and easily. Public bills, however, are another story. These are the bills we read about in the newspaper and see on television; these are what we will be concerned with here.

Before we trace the life history of a bill, we should note that, for the vast majority of bills, life barely begins before it ends. Most expert estimates calculate that only one bill in eight gets serious consideration; and even for those that do, passage is by no means certain. On the average, of all the thousands of bills introduced in one two-year Congress, only about 4 percent become law! There are several reasons why a bill's chances are so remote. In part, it's because Congress just does not have the time to consider very many. It is also because congressional leaders may know from the start the bill has little or no chance for the necessary support and success, and thus dismiss it. Finally, it is because even those bills that do have widespread support must travel a very rocky road to become law.

First of all, a bill must be written, or drafted. Sometimes congressmen will draft bills themselves, but usually it is done by an interest group or executive agency. The reason for this is that these highly specialized groups and agencies have a thorough knowledge of the bill's subject. The congressman, on the other hand, usually doesn't have the time to achieve the same level of expertise. As a result, though the congressman often will work closely with the experts and give them his ideas, it is the latter who usually supply the enormous effort necessary to research and write a good bill.

For example, perhaps a team of experts from the federal Environmental Protection Agency wants to pass a law to reduce pollution in rivers. After discussing the idea—and getting the support of a prominent member of the Senate Committee on Environment and Public Works—the experts will draft the bill. Then they turn it over to the senator, who may suggest some minor changes. Once they agree on all the provisions, the bill is ready to be introduced.

Except for money bills, which the Constitution says must begin in the House, a bill may start in either chamber of Congress. To get started, it must be introduced by a member or group of members. In the House, a bill is introduced merely by dropping it in the hopper on the clerk's desk. It then is given a number, H.R. 1, H.R. 2, etc. (H.R. meaning House of Representatives), printed, and distributed to all the members. A copy will appear in the *Congressional Record*, the official daily digest of all that goes on in Congress.

In the Senate, the procedure for introducing a bill is somewhat more formal. After getting recognition from the presiding officer, the senator who wants to introduce it stands up and makes a brief case for why the bill is needed. After the bill is taken by a messenger to the rostrum, it is given a number, in this case S.1, S. 2, etc., printed, and distributed.

The next step is for the bill to be referred to the appropriate committee by the Speaker of the House and the majority leader in the Senate. Usually it's obvious which committee a bill should go to; farm bills go to agriculture committees, spending bills to appropriations committees, and a labor bill to the labor committees.* Sometimes, however, when a bill

---

*Certain committees, which do basically the same things, are given different names in the House and Senate. For example, the House Agriculture Committee is virtually the same as the Senate Committee on Agriculture and Forestry. Similarly, the House Ways and Means Committee serves the same function as the Senate Finance Committee.

might fall under the jurisdiction of more than one committee, the leaders of each house can exercise great influence by directing it to the committee where it has the best chance for positive action.

Such was the case in 1963, when the Civil Rights Act was introduced. Ordinarily, the bill would seem appropriate for the House Judiciary Committee. However, the majority leaders in the House were well aware that the chairman of that committee, James Eastland of Mississippi, was dead set against the bill. So, citing a little-known clause in the bill, the leaders were able, *justifiably,* to place the bill with the House Commerce Committee, where it had a much better chance to pass. Thanks to similar maneuvering in the Senate, the bill became law in 1964.

Once a bill is in committee, its fate depends largely on the chairman. Before we consider what process the bill goes through in committee, let's get acquainted with these all-powerful chairmen.

First of all, the committee chairmen always are members of the majority party. If, after an election, their party is no longer in a majority, then they are dethroned. If not, then they retain their staggering influence over bills that come to their committees. That influence includes the power to:

- *pigeonhole,* or refuse to consider, any bill of which they do not approve
- set the committee's agenda, deciding when and what will be taken up
- appoint subcommittee chairmen, as well as all subcommittee members
- decide whether a *hearing*—an open session in which various experts are invited to talk about matters related to the bill—should be conducted
- hire and supervise the committee staff, which may consist of experts, researchers, lawyers, and clerks
- manage the bill on the House floor, and decide which

committee members shall speak on its behalf.

Now let's see just how committee chairmen acquire that power.

Until the 1970s, committee chairmen were automatically chosen on the basis of seniority. Thus, the majority party member who served on the committee longest got the chair. This method of choosing chairmen caused much controversy. Some people argued that it was unfair to highly qualified members who simply did not have enough years in the chamber. Opponents of seniority also asserted that the system was completely arbitrary, and that it tended to install chairmen who did not reflect the majority interests of Congress.* Other detractors pointed to the advanced age of many chairmen—more than two-thirds of whom, a recent study showed, were sixty or older—and claimed they were not open to new ideas.

On the other side, defenders of seniority said the system ensured experienced leadership, and prevented nasty battles about who should be chairman.

Amid this controversy, the seniority system among House Democrats came tumbling down in a series of moves in the early 1970s, culminating in 1975, when the power to nominate chairmen was given to a special committee. The committee then would turn its nominations over to a caucus, which would have the final say. When it was over, three powerful committee chairmen had been toppled.

The upshot of this move, along with a similar decision by the Senate Republicans, was to warn committee chairmen that they could not rely solely on seniority to remain in power. They now would be held accountable for their performances, and any abuses of power within their committee.

---

*To support this point, seniority critics pointed out that a disproportionate number of chairmen come from the Deep South. Why? Because, for a long time, the South was such a solid one-party area that its congressmen kept on getting reelected—and building seniority.

Although the seniority system still plays a big part in the awarding of chairmanships, the chairmen are no longer the "untouchables" they once were.

With this background information on the chairmen, let's return to what happens to the bill in committee. The chairman, as we now know, can terminate the process immediately by pigeonholing the bill if he believes there is no need for such a law. If, on the other hand, he approves of the bill, then the wheels start turning. The chairman might bring up the bill for consideration at a committee meeting and then schedule a hearing. What is much more common, though, is for the chairman to refer the bill to one of his subcommittees. Once he does this, the ball is in the subcommittee chairman's court. He, too, may have the power to delay or pigeonhole the bill, depending on how much independence he's given by the committee chairman. Chances are, however, that if the chairman is strongly in favor of the measure, then the subcommittee chairman will keep it alive.

Assuming the subcommittee chairman is in favor of the bill, then it's time to get some expert opinion on the matter. A hearing is arranged so the subcommittee can question knowledgeable people about the impact the bill would have. Fellow congressmen, lobbyists, and representatives from executive agencies all are likely candidates for testifying at a hearing. Sometimes, if the bill is of national concern and at all controversial, then public hearings are conducted.

Apart from their immense value in helping a subcommittee get all the facts, hearings can also be used as a means to drum up support for the bill's cause. By attracting newspaper and television coverage for its hearing, the committee can make a strong case for a bill and improve its chances of being passed on the floor of the chamber.

Once the hearing is over, and the subcommittee has gathered all the information it needs, the next step is the *markup*. In this executive meeting, which is closed to the press and public, the subcommittee painstakingly pores over the bill, adding, deleting, changing the language, and generally "marking" it up. The bill may change substantially during the markup, or it might not change much at all. It depends on how much the subcommittee chairman feels he has to compromise in order to get support from the majority of the committee.

Following the markup session, the subcommittee votes on the bill. If it is passed, which is almost always the case, since most large differences are hammered out in markup, it proceeds back to the full committee. Then the full committee votes on it, *reporting* its findings to the chamber. In voting, the committee virtually always follows the lead of the subcommittee; bills rarely are reported unfavorably, since the committee can "kill" the bill merely by refusing to act on it.

Let's assume, then, that the full committee reports the bill favorably to the chamber. Along with the final version of the bill, the committee sends a written report, summarizing its views on the matter. Sometimes, those in disagreement with the committee's findings will file their views in a separate report.

Now back in the chamber where it was first introduced, the bill is placed on a calendar. In the Senate, the scheduling of bills is controlled by the majority party; in the House, by a powerful group called the *Rules Committee*. Formed in 1880, the Rules Committee was created to be a traffic cop for the House. By scheduling and controlling the flow of bills, and placing rules on bills regarding how long the issue should be debated and whether amendments, or changes, should be permitted, the Rules Committee was supposed to make the legislative process go smoothly and efficiently.

In practice, though, the Rules Committee has been more than a traffic cop. By simply refusing to grant a bill a "rule," it actually can kill the bill. In the early 1960s, the Rules Committee killed a number of major bills in this fashion— bills that had widespread support in the House. As a result of these abuses of power, the House adopted measures to curtail the Rules Committee's power; one such measure was the so-called "21-day rule," which authorizes the Speaker to bring a bill to the House floor if the Rules Committee has not issued a rule within twenty-one days of receiving the bill.*

In spite of these changes, the Rules Committee remains one of the most powerful committees in the House. It can still block bills it doesn't favor, and for those that it does favor, it can issue a closed rule, which means no amendments can be made on the House floor.

Once a bill has succeeded in getting a rule, it proceeds to the House floor. In the Senate, as we know, the bill does not need a rule; it comes to the floor at the time it was scheduled by the majority party leaders. Provided a quorum—presence of at least half the members of the chamber—is reached, debate on the bill begins.

The debate phase, too, differs in the House and the Senate. Because of its large membership, the House is limited in its time for debate by the Rules Committee; on matters of national importance, debate usually is restricted to four to eight hours. The Senate, on the other hand, has no such limitations. Senators are permitted to talk and talk and talk some more. This freedom enables senators to thoroughly consider every aspect of a bill; it also enables them to try to block a bill by using a *filibuster*. A filibuster is a tactic in which a senator opposed to a bill will literally attempt to

---

*Aside from the "21-day rule," the House has other more complex ways to bypass the Rules Committee. In practice however, they are used very rarely, which is an accurate measure of just how powerful the Rules Committee is.

talk a bill to death. By holding the floor—or talking—for hours on end, the filibustering senator and other opponents hope to convince their colleagues to scrap the bill. Sometimes it works; sometimes it doesn't. If the supporters of the bill refuse to yield, they can keep the Senate in session indefinitely, thereby forcing their filibustering fellows to hold the floor until they're ready to drop. One memorable filibuster came in 1957, when Senator Strom Thurmond of South Carolina kept talking for twenty-four hours and eighteen minutes.

The only way a filibuster can be stopped is if sixty senators vote to cut off debate. This measure is known as *cloture*. It is not used too often, though, since many senators feel they might want to filibuster someday, and they would not want a cloture imposed on them. One notable instance when cloture *was* invoked, however, was in the early 1960s, when supporters of the Civil Rights Act cut short the debate and succeeded in passing the legislation.

Regardless of how long the debate over the bill continues, many visitors who watch the proceedings in the gallery overhanging each chamber (you can get a gallery pass from your congressman if you'd like to see the proceedings for yourself) are somewhat disappointed by the often sparse attendance and uninspired discussion. In many cases, congressmen are sure of how they stand on a bill, and don't feel the need to be present for the duration of the debate. They might slip back into their offices for a while, or they might stay on the floor and read over important papers.

However, once the general debate is concluded and the amending process begins (unless, in the House, the bill is under closed rule), both attendance and interest pick up markedly. Summoned by a buzzer system that sounds through Capitol buildings and tells congressmen that a vote is being held, a quorum is needed, or the amendments are being considered, congressmen will pour into their respective floors. This amending process gives congressmen a chance to discuss and make changes to the bill; it is the time a congressman who is against the bill might propose a change, which, if accepted, would convince him to change his stand.

The role of the *floor manager*—the congressman, usually the committee or subcommittee chairman who is trying to get it passed—is vital during the amending period. He must decide just how many concessions he needs to make in order to get the bill passed. If he thinks the bill will pass by itself, he will oppose most amendments. If he isn't so sure, he might go along with the proposed changes.

After each amendment is debated (in the House, opponents and supporters of the amendment are given only five minutes to state their case; in the Senate, again, it is unlimited), a vote is held. After all amendments have been debated and voted on, the members vote on the bill itself. If the majority of those present vote in favor of the bill, it has successfully passed through that chamber.

Is that it? Is the bill now law? Not by a long shot. So far, the bill has only made it through one house. Now it must survive the same long and hazardous process in the other house. That means it must be introduced, referred to committee, analyzed in a committee or subcommittee hearing, revised in the markup session, reported to the floor, placed on a calendar (or, if it started in the Senate, get a rule from the House Rules Committee), undergo general floor debate and the amendment debates, and finally, voted on.

Let's assume the bill has passed through both houses. Now is it law? Not quite. As the bill went through the twisted path in each house, it probably underwent different changes in each. They might be major changes, or they might be minor ones. In any case, to merge the two versions into one, the bill must go to a conference committee, a panel which consists of members of each house. After this committee agrees on the exact provisions and wording of the bill, it is sent back to each house for final approval. From there, it goes to the man in the White House—the president of the United States.

If the president signs the bill, it becomes law. If the president chooses to not sign, or veto, the bill, it goes back to Congress. In order to override the president's veto, each house of Congress must pass the bill by a two-thirds majority. Even if one house is just one vote short of that majority, then the bill dies. For this reason, overriding a veto is very difficult. In the administration of President Gerald Ford, Congress managed to override only twelve of Mr. Ford's seventy-two vetoes.

So there we have it . . . the not-so-simple road a bill must travel to become a law. With all the different twists and turns and pitfalls a bill must survive to reach the end of that road, it's not at all surprising that so few bills manage to make it.

A Day In the Life

Judging by the time and energy that go into the making of each and every law, it's a wonder our congressmen have time for anything else. Indeed, the countless hours of studying, researching, discussing, consulting, debating, amending, and finally, voting, on every piece of legislation, would seem a full-time job in itself. But, for our congressmen, that's only a part of their daily grind on the Hill. After they make the laws, they must make sure the administration is carrying them out effectively. And they must make sure that the taxpayers' money—our money, which we have entrusted them to spend—is being used wisely. On top of all that, our congressmen must never forget about the people who put them in Washington. That means answering letters, providing information, running errands, making trips back home, and taking great pains to keep a finger on the pulse of their constituents. Can a congressman do all this in one day? No way. He can only weigh his priorities, try his best, and plunge ahead. Let's see how he might do it.

HOW A BILL BECOMES A LAW

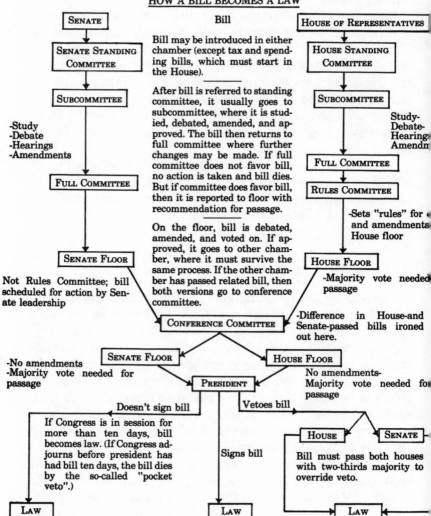

Bill

Bill may be introduced in either chamber (except tax and spending bills, which must start in the House).

After bill is referred to standing committee, it usually goes to subcommittee, where it is studied, debated, amended, and approved. The bill then returns to full committee where further changes may be made. If full committee does not favor bill, no action is taken and bill dies. But if committee does favor bill, then it is reported to floor with recommendation for passage.

On the floor, bill is debated, amended, and voted on. If approved, it goes to other chamber, where it must survive the same process. If the other chamber has passed related bill, then both versions go to conference committee.

SENATE

SENATE STANDING COMMITTEE

SUBCOMMITTEE

-Study
-Debate
-Hearings
-Amendments

FULL COMMITTEE

SENATE FLOOR

Not Rules Committee; bill scheduled for action by Senate leadership

HOUSE OF REPRESENTATIVES

HOUSE STANDING COMMITTEE

SUBCOMMITTEE

Study-
Debate-
Hearings
Amendm

FULL COMMITTEE

RULES COMMITTEE

-Sets "rules" for
and amendments
House floor

HOUSE FLOOR

-Majority vote needed
passage

-Difference in House-and Senate-passed bills ironed out here.

CONFERENCE COMMITTEE

SENATE FLOOR   **HOUSE FLOOR**

-No amendments
-Majority vote needed for passage

No amendments-
Majority vote needed for passage

PRESIDENT

Doesn't sign bill   Vetoes bill

If Congress is in session for more than ten days, bill becomes law. (If Congress adjourns before president has had bill ten days, the bill dies by the so-called "pocket veto".)

Signs bill

HOUSE   **SENATE**

Bill must pass both houses with two-thirds majority to override veto.

LAW   **LAW**   **LAW**

It's seven o'clock in the morning. Along with a quick breakfast and a couple of cups of coffee, Representative Preston Peabody scans his morning newspaper and a copy of the previous day's *Congressional Record*. He knows that keeping informed of all that goes on on Capitol Hill is a huge chore, so he relies on the *Record* to help him do it. As a freshman, it's especially important for Peabody, since he hasn't yet developed the far-reaching network of sources and contacts that senior members have.

He arrives at his office shortly after eight. He promptly burrows into a stack of mail—the mail he will answer personally. The letters deemed less important will be handled by the staff. Quickly but carefully, he dictates his replies. He is mildly disturbed by a "crackpot" letter from a cynical voter, asking him if he is "enjoying his vacation in Washington." Peabody's brief but pointed response: "I welcome you to come to Washington and follow me around for a day, and then see what you think of my vacation." The next letter, by contrast, is very uplifting. Composed by a knowledgeable and well-informed constituent, it praises Peabody for his voting record in support of transportation funds for the district.

After hammering out responses to twenty or so letters, he takes time out to meet with his staff. They go over the day's busy agenda—the meetings, appointments, the casework, and the legislative homework that must be tackled. A top aide hands him the research materials Peabody requested for a bill he is considering. As the brief conference disperses, Peabody thinks how fortunate he is to have assembled such a top-notch staff in his very first term.

A fellow representative appears on the scene, and the two retreat into Peabody's office. They discuss the merits of a bill that recently has been referred to their Public Works and Transportation Committee. An aide knocks on the door, and informs Peabody that a reporter and photographer from his district's newspaper are waiting for him. Peabody apologetically tells his colleague they'll have to continue their discussion later. A half hour later, the reporter has his story and the photographer has his pictures. Peabody is looking forward to seeing it in Sunday's paper. He knows publicity can only do him good.

An aide reminds him that it is nearly ten o'clock. Peabody has four different committee and subcommittee meetings at ten. Such conflicts are common. Today, Peabody is attending an important subcommittee hearing of the Interior and Insular Affairs Committee. For two hours, he and his colleagues question a panel of environmental experts on why a bill to pass more stringent air pollution standards is necessary. By his line of questioning, it is obvious Peabody has done his homework. He impresses the senior members with his command of the subject.

The hearing adjourns a few minutes before noon, and Peabody heads over to the Capitol, where the daily floor sessions are about to begin. As the clock strikes twelve, the Speaker raps his gavel, bringing the House to order. Peabody takes a seat on one side of the aisle which divides the large chamber. Republicans, by custom, sit on the left side of the aisle, and Democrats on the right. The arrangement is similar in the Senate chamber, except, since there are only one hundred members, each Senator has his own desk.

During a floor debate on an appropriations bill, Peabody checks his watch and hurriedly dashes downstairs to the restaurant, where he is to meet a group of senior citizens from his district at one o'clock. A few minutes late, Peabody locates the group and apologizes for his tardiness. Near the end of the luncheon, a buzzer sounds in the restaurant. Peabody excuses himself and goes upstairs to vote on a bill. It wasn't too important or controversial a bill, and Peabody knew how he would vote on it. That's why he didn't feel the need to sit in on the debate. His vote recorded, he hurries back downstairs, apologizes once more, and thanks the folks for stopping by.

Seeing he has a little time before a major bill comes up for discussion, Peabody quickly heads back to his office to make a few phone calls and pick up the messages from the people who tried to reach him when he was out. Along the way, he runs into a lobbyist from a business organization. The lobbyist wants to discuss with Peabody the negative effect that the proposed air pollution legislation would have on the local business and economy. But Peabody is in too much of a hurry to give much thought to the lobbyist's opinions; he makes an appointment with the lobbyist for early the next week.

Back at the office, Peabody returns a couple of phone calls and contacts the Federal Housing Authority to straighten out a loan problem a constituent has been having. As he grabs his coat, a fistful of phone messages yet to be answered, and hustles back to the floor, he bumps into a family from the district. He stops and chats with them for a short while, but tells them he must get to the Capitol. He instructs an aide to show the family around Washington.

Back on the floor, a key energy bill is being hotly debated. Peabody carefully reads the committee report on the bill, then sits down with a committee member to quietly discuss its details. He is not yet sure how he will vote, but since he's got some time before amendments are considered, he ducks out to a phone booth to attend to the messages, handling several more constituent problems and talking with various executive agencies. After twenty productive minutes, he goes back to the floor. Peabody's timing is perfect. Amendments are just about to be considered.

Suddenly, the House floor comes alive. Members file in by the dozens. It's clear the whips for both parties have done their jobs in getting members to the floor. The debate is spirited, as supporters and opponents of proposed amendments express their views. Knowing the final vote on the bill will be close, the floor manager agrees to a couple of minor amendments, but steadfastly refuses any major changes, which he thinks would defeat the bill's purpose.

Peabody is troubled by one question throughout the debate, and finally, he rises and asks one of the spokesmen to yield the floor so Peabody can make his point. He does so, and is impressed with the answer from the bill's supporters. He decides, after thoughtful consideration, to vote in favor of the measure.

Finally, all the amendments have been debated and voted on. Peabody checks his watch. It's after six o'clock; it has been a long session. Peabody had hoped to check back into the office for an hour or so to answer and sign letters, and get back to the steady stream of phone callers who inevitably tried to reach him in the afternoon. But he knows he won't have anywhere near that much time; he's supposed to attend a dinner party at seven o'clock in honor of a prominent labor leader from a big city in his state.

But Peabody can't think of all that now. It's time for the long-awaited vote. Tension mounts in the historic chamber. The representatives cast their decisions—aye or nay—which are recorded on an electronic scoreboard over the visitor's gallery. The vote is close, but the bill passes. Peabody is pleased as he quickly departs for his office, where he has time only to sign a batch of letters and place two important calls. Nowhere near finished but out of time, Peabody phones his wife and tells her he'll meet her at the dinner.

Although Peabody enjoys the function, and engages in some enlightening political inside talk, he looks forward to getting home. He has been going a long time. He and his wife finally get in about 10:30.

But before he can turn in, he pores over a bundle of research documents he needs to be familiar with for a hearing tomorrow. He reads, makes notes, and writes down questions. Then he draws up a list of the things to which he must give top priority tomorrow. On top of the list is a reminder to have an aide make a plane reservation for him and his wife. They are going back to the district for the coming weekend. Peabody hasn't been in Congress for very long, but already he has learned the importance of answering the mail, running the errands, and keeping in touch with the folks back home. Trips home every month or so—especially in the "off-year"—can work wonders. Peabody has discovered that's the best time to talk to people, attend lunches and dinners, make speeches, and show the people he is interested in their needs and concerns. There's no campaign pressure, no other candidate to worry about.

As he eases into bed, Peabody thinks about the full slate of activities he has planned for his weekend at home. A handful of meetings, a luncheon, a dinner, and a speech at a high school graduation ceremony. Then the words of a wise old colleague dance into his head: "First take care of your district. Become a statesman later."

With that, the day is over for Representative Preston Peabody.

Epiloge

The Branch of the People

WE LIVE IN A TIME when disillusionment with government is at an all-time high. In late 1979, a poll taken by *The New York Times* and the Columbia Broadcasting System (CBS) showed that a mere 29 percent of those interviewed believed that our government could be trusted to "do what is right." Although the poll didn't single out Congress, it's reasonable to assume that the American people are as unhappy with

Congress as any other part of our government.

We don't have to look far to find evidence of this wide-spread disaffection. In the 1978 House elections, one esti-mate stated that roughly 65 percent of our nation's eligible voters decided not to bother. For Senate elections, the turn-out was not much better. This means that fewer than two out of five adults cared enough to take the five minutes it requires to vote. This does not bode well for our democracy.

When so many millions of people drop out, when so many simply don't care who represents them in our government, then our democratic system is not functioning as it is sup-posed to. The origin of the word democracy, remember, means "people rule;" not "two out of five rule."

There can be little doubt that Congress has brought some of this disrepute on itself. Over the last ten years, we've been bombarded with dozens of stories about the misdeeds of our public officials: shady campaign financing, trips at public expense, income tax evasion, even alleged vote-buy-ing. Some of these stories were true, some weren't. In any case, it makes people angry. And they get even angrier when they read that Congress recently voted itself a hefty pay raise—to $60,663—at a time when millions of Ameri-cans cannot find work. It leads people to think that Congress is looking out for itself, but not for the people it is supposed to represent.

While all congressmen may not be as conscientious and dedicated as our imaginary Preston Peabody, it's hardly fair to point fingers at all 535 of them. The number of dishonest and corrupt congressmen is infinitesimal compared to the number who are earnestly trying to serve their constituents to the best of their abilities.

What Congress is, really, is a mirror of the American people. Though the overwhelming majority of its members are honest people with the best of intentions, there is bound to be a few bad apples in the barrel. That's where we, the voters, come in. It's up to us to get rid of the "bad apples."

These people are our voice in government. We elected them
. . . we can "un-elect" them.

But not if we don't vote. By not caring enough to vote, we
are only making things worse. It's like saying, "Go ahead
and do what you want. We won't hold you accountable."

The only way Congress can get better is if we assert our
roles in the democratic process. That means being informed,
responsible citizens. It also means voting.

Our congressmen are the only federal officials whom we
elect directly. They are our public servants, our direct link
in government. In 1789, our founding fathers created Congress and declared it "the branch of the people."

Now, nearly two hundred years later, it is up to every one
of us to keep it that way.

Appendix I

A Guide to Writing Your Congressman

LET'S ASSUME YOU have a question, problem, suggestion, or opinion that you want to contact your representative or senators about. How should you do it?

First, let's see how you should *not* do it. Telephoning your congressmen is always a hit-or-miss proposition, because they are in and out of the office so much. Showing up at the office, either at home or in Washington, also may be disappointing; if you do get to see him, there's a good bet he'll be too harried to give you much time. A telegram is quick and easy, but for the same reasons, congressmen tend not to pay it much mind.

Just about all congressmen agree that the best way to reach them is by writing a letter. You don't have to have a highly original idea or a grand plan to cure our nation's ills for your congressman to be interested in what you're writing about. Indeed, if there's anything a congressman needs, it's a sharper focus on what the "typical" people he serves are thinking. He is always getting mail from high-powered interest groups and organizations; he needs to hear more from you, your friends, and your family. Your congressman will be pleased and grateful that you are concerned enough to take the time to write.

Here are a few guidelines to follow in composing your letter:

- Be neat. Whether you are typing or writing longhand, make an extra effort to be neat. It makes it easier for your congressman to read, and besides, messy letters create bad impressions and probably will be given less consideration.

126

- Be clear. Take the time to organize your thoughts before you put the pen to paper. The end result will be well worth the few minutes of planning.
- Be brief. Try not to ramble. Simply say what you want to say, then wrap it up. In most cases, a page or two should be plenty.
- Be forthright. If you are writing to take issue with a bill or law, or to propose a new one, don't be afraid to support your arguments with facts. Who knows, you may be telling your congressman something he is not aware of. Besides, a simple statement of opinion, without anything to back it up, will not mean much. A sentence such as, "I think pollution stinks," by itself is too general to carry any weight.

  If, on the other hand, you go into more detail, your case will be much better: "The other day I went to go swimming in Beachfront Bay. When I got there, I saw a sign saying that the bay was polluted and not safe to swim in anymore. This makes me angry. I have been swimming there for many years. Isn't there something we can do to stop pollution so we can still enjoy our natural resources?"
- Be polite. Assuming you decide to write because you are disturbed about something, don't start hurling insults at your congressman. That won't do any good. State your viewpoint as best you can. If you don't approve of the way your congressman has represented you, and you're not convinced by his reasoning, then you may want to support another candidate in the next election. And, finally, it never hurts to drop your congressman a line to say you think he's doing a good job. If you're a student of Congress, and that's what you think, why not let him know? You might make his whole day!

Here is the proper form and addresses for your congressmen:

Representatives	*Senators*
The Honorable Preston Peabody House Office Building Washington, D.C. 20515	The Honorable Steven Young Senate Office Building Washington, D.C. 20510
Dear Representative Peabody:	Dear Senator Young:

A parting note: If you want a reply, don't forget to include your address!

Appendix II

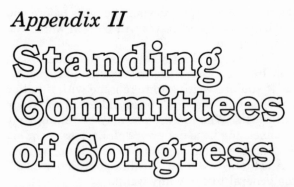

Standing Committees of Congress

House of Representatives	*Senate*
Agriculture	Agriculture, Nutrition, and Forestry
Appropriations	Appropriations
Armed Services	Armed Services
Banking, Finance, and Urban Affairs	Banking, Finance, and Urban Affairs
Budget	Budget
District of Columbia	Commerce, Science, and Transportation
Education and Labor	Energy and Natural Resources
Government Operations	Environment and Public Works
House Administration	Finance
Interior and Insular Affairs	Foreign Relations
Foreign Affairs	Governmental Affairs
Interstate and Foreign Commerce	Human Resources
Judiciary	Judiciary
Merchant Marine and Fisheries	Rules and Administration
Post Office and Civil Service	Small Business
Public Works	Veterans' Affairs
Rules	
Science and Technology	
Small Business	
Ways and Means	

Appendix III

Constitution of the United States

(Key Selections)

WE THE PEOPLE of the United States, in Order to form a more perfect Union, establish Justice, insure domestic Tranquility, provide for the common defence, promote the general Welfare, and secure the Blessings of Liberty to ourselves and our Posterity, do ordain and establish this Constitution for the United States of America.

ARTICLE I

Section 1. All legislative Powers herein granted shall be vested in a Congress of the United States, which shall consist of a Senate and House of Representatives.

Section 2. The House of Representatives shall be composed of Members chosen every second Year by the People of the several States, and the Electors in each State shall have the Qualifications requisite for Electors of the most numerous Branch of the State Legislature.

No Person shall be a Representative who shall not have attained to the age of twenty five Years, and been seven Years a Citizen of the United States, and who shall not, when elected, be an Inhabitant of that State in which he shall be chosen.

[Representatives and direct Taxes shall be apportioned among the several States which may be included within this Union, according to their respective Numbers, which shall be determined by adding to the whole Number of free Persons, including those bound to Service for a Term of Years, and excluding Indians not taxed, three fifths of all other Persons.][1] The actual Enumeration shall be made within three Years after the first Meeting of the Congress of the United States, and within every subsequent Term of ten Years, in such Manner as they shall by Law direct. The Number of Representatives shall not exceed one for every thirty Thousand, but each State shall have at Least one Representative; and until such enumeration shall be made, the State of New Hampshire shall be entitled to chuse three, Massachusetts eight, Rhode-Island and Providence Plantations one, Connecticut five, New-York six, New Jersey four, Pennsylvania eight, Delaware one, Maryland six, Virginia ten, North Carolina five, South Carolina five, and Georgia three.

When vacancies happen in the Representation from any State, the Executive Authority thereof shall issue Writs of Election to fill such Vacancies.

The House of Representatives shall chuse their Speaker and other Officers; and shall have the sole Power of Impeachment.

Section 3. The Senate of the United States shall be composed of two Senators from each State, [chosen by the Legislature thereof,][2] for six Years; and each Senator shall have one Vote.

Immediately after they shall be assembled in Consequence of the first Election, they shall be divided as equally as may be into three Classes. The Seats of the Senators of the first Class shall be vacated at the Expiration of the second Year, of the second Class at the Expiration of the fourth Year, and of the third Class at the Expiration of the sixth Year, so that one third may be chosen every second Year; [and if Vacancies happen by Resignation, or otherwise, during the Recess of the Legislature of any State, the Executive thereof may make temporary Appointments until the next Meeting of the Legislature, which shall then fill such Vacancies.][3]

No Person shall be a Senator who shall not have attained to the Age of thirty Years, and been nine Years a Citizen of the United States, and who shall not, when elected, be an Inhabitant of that State for which he shall be chosen.

The Vice President of the United States shall be President of the Senate, but shall have no Vote, unless they be equally divided.

The Senate shall chuse their other Officers, and also a President pro tempore, in the Absence of the Vice President, or when he shall exercise the Office of President of the United States.

The Senate shall have the sole Power to try all Impeachments. When sitting for that Purpose, they shall be on Oath or Affirmation. When the President of the United States is tried the Chief Justice shall preside: And no Person shall be convicted without the Concurrence of two thirds of the Members present.

Judgment in Cases of Impeachment shall not extend further than to removal from Office, and disqualification to hold and enjoy any Office of honor, Trust or Profit under the United States: but the Party convicted shall nevertheless be liable and subject to Indictment, Trial, Judgment and Punishment, according to Law.

Section 4. The Times, Places and Manner of holding Elections for Senators and Representatives, shall be prescribed in each State by the Legislature thereof; but the Congress may at any time by Law make or alter such Regulations, except as to the Places of chusing Senators.

The Congress shall assemble at least once in every Year, and such Meeting shall [be on the first Monday in December],⁴ unless they shall by Law appoint a different Day.

Section 5. Each House shall be the Judge of the Elections, Returns and Qualifications of its own Members, and a Majority of each shall constitute a Quorum to do Business; but a smaller Number may adjourn from day to day, and may be authorized to compel the Attendance of absent Members, in such Manner, and under such Penalties as each House may provide.

Each House may determine the Rules of its Proceedings, punish its Members for disorderly Behaviour, and, with the Concurrence of two thirds, expel a Member.

Each House shall keep a Journal of its Proceedings, and from time to time publish the same, excepting such Parts as may in their Judgment require Secrecy; and the Yeas and Nays of the Members of either House on any question shall, at the Desire of one fifth of those Present, be entered on the Journal.

Neither House, during the Session of Congress, shall, without the Consent of the other, adjourn for more than three days, nor to any other Place than that in which the two Houses shall be sitting.

Section 6. The Senators and Representatives shall receive a

Compensation for their Services, to be ascertained by Law, and paid out of the Treasury of the United States. They shall in all Cases, except Treason, Felony and Breach of the Peace, be privileged from Arrest during their Attendance at the Session of their respective Houses, and in going to and returning from the same; and for any Speech or Debate in either House, they shall not be questioned in any other Place.

No Senator or Representative shall, during the Time for which he was elected, be appointed to any civil Office under the Authority of the United States, which shall have been created, or the Emoluments whereof shall have been encreased during such time; and no Person holding any Office under the United States, shall be a Member of either House during his Continuance in Office.

Section 7. All Bills for raising Revenue shall originate in the House of Representatives; but the Senate may propose or concur with amendments as on other Bills.

Every Bill which shall have passed the House of Representatives and the Senate, shall, before it become a Law, be presented to the President of the United States; If he approve he shall sign it, but if not he shall return it, with his Objections to that House in which it shall have originated, who shall enter the Objections at large on their Journal, and proceed to reconsider it. If after such Reconsideration two thirds of that House shall agree to pass the Bill, it shall be sent, together with the Objections, to the other House, by which it shall likewise be reconsidered, and if approved by two thirds of that House, it shall become a Law. But in all such Cases the Votes of both Houses shall be determined by yeas and Nays, and the Names of the Persons voting for and against the Bill shall be entered on the Journal of each House respectively. If any Bill shall not be returned by the President within ten Days (Sunday excepted) after it shall have been presented to him, the Same shall be a Law, in like Manner as if he had signed it, unless the Congress by their Adjournment prevent its Return, in which Case it shall not be a Law.

Every Order, Resolution, or Vote to which the Concurrence of the Senate and House of Representatives may be necessary (except on a question of Adjournment) shall be presented to the President of the United States; and before the Same shall take

Effect, shall be approved by him, or being disapproved by him,
shall be repassed by two thirds of the Senate and House of Representatives, according to the Rules and Limitations prescribed in
the Case of a Bill.

Section 8. The Congress shall have Power To lay and collect
Taxes, Duties, Imposts and Excises, to pay the Debts and provide
for the common Defence and general Welfare of the United
States; but all Duties, Imposts and Excises shall be uniform
throughout the United States;

To borrow Money on the credit of the United States;

To regulate Commerce with foreign Nations, and among the
several States, and with the Indian Tribes;

To establish an uniform Rule of Naturalization, and uniform
Laws on the subject of Bankruptcies throughout the United
States;

To coin Money, regulate the Value thereof, and of foreign Coin,
and fix the Standard of Weights and Measures;

To provide for the Punishment of counterfeiting the Securities
and current Coin of the United States;

To establish Post Offices and post Roads;

To promote the Progress of Science and useful Arts, by securing
for limited Times to Authors and Inventors the exclusive Right to
their respective Writings and Discoveries;

To constitute Tribunals inferior to the supreme Court;

To define and punish Piracies and Felonies commited on the
high Seas, and Offences against the Law of Nations;

To declare War, grant Letters of Marque and Reprisal, and
make Rules concerning Captures on Land and Water;

To raise and support Armies, but no Appropriation of Money to
that Use shall be for a longer Term than two Years;

To provide and maintain a Navy;

To make Rules for the Government and Regulation of the land
and naval Forces;

To provide for calling forth the Militia to execute the Laws of
the Union, suppress Insurrections and repel Invasions;

To provide for organizing, arming, and disciplining, the Militia, and for governing such Part of them as may be employed in the Service of the United States, reserving to the States respectively, the Appointment of the Officers, and the Authority of training the Militia according to the discipline prescribed by Congress;

To exercise exclusive Legislation in all Cases whatsoever, over such District (not exceeding ten Miles square) as may, by Cession of Particular States, and the Acceptance of Congress, become the Seat of the Government of the United States, and to exercise like Authority over all Places purchased by the Consent of the Legislature of the State in which the Same shall be, for the Erection of Forts, Magazines, Arsenals, dock-Yards, and other needful Buildings;—And

To make all Laws which shall be necessary and proper for carrying into Execution the foregoing Powers, and all other Powers vested by this Constitution in the Government of the United States, or in any Department or Officer thereof.

Section 9. The Migration or Importation of such Persons as any of the States now existing shall think proper to admit, shall not be prohibited by the Congress prior to the Year one thousand eight hundred and eight, but a Tax or duty may be imposed on such Importation, not exceeding ten dollars for each Person.

The Privilege of the Writ of Habeas Corpus shall not be suspended, unless when in Cases of Rebellion or Invasion the public Safety may require it.

No Bill of Attainder or ex post facto Law shall be passed.

No Capitation, or other direct, Tax shall be laid, unless in Proportion to the Census of Enumeration herein before directed to be taken.[5]

No Tax or Duty shall be laid on Articles exported from any State.

No Preference shall be given by any Regulation of Commerce or Revenue to the Ports of one State over those of another; nor shall Vessels bound to, or from, one State, be obliged to enter, clear or pay Duties in another.

No Money shall be drawn from the Treasury, but in Consequence of Appropriations made by Law; and a regular Statement and Account of the Receipts and Expenditures of all public Money shall be published from time to time.

No Title of Nobility shall be granted by the United States: And no Person holding any Office of Profit or Trust under them, shall, without the Consent of the Congress, accept of any present, Emolument, Office, or Title, of any kind whatever, from any King, Prince or foreign State.

Glossary

Amendment: A change in a bill. Also, a revision in the United States Constitution.

Anti-Federalists: A political party, led by Thomas Jefferson in the late 1700s, that was firmly opposed to a strong federal government.

Apportionment: The distribution of congressional districts among the states.

Apprenticeship: A folkway of Congress suggesting that newcomers should learn their way around and carefully study senior members before plunging into their duties.

Appropriation: A law that authorizes money to be spent by the federal treasury.

Bandwagon: A political campaign that is far in front of the opposition. Thus, *jumping on the bandwagon* is to join the campaign of the candidate who seems to be the likely winner. Derives from the old practice of candidates to stage colorful parades; leading the parade was a musical band, perched on a large wagon. As a show of support for the candidate, local politicians would leap onto the "bandwagon."

Bicameral legislature: A lawmaking branch of government that has two separate parts, or houses. The American Congress is a bicameral legislature, consisting of the Senate and the House of Representatives.

Bill: A proposed law. There are two types of bills, public and private. A private bill is designed to help a private citizen. A public bill is designed to make broad changes which affect many people, and sometimes the entire country.

Candidate: A person seeking public office.

Capitol Hill: The home of our Congress; a small hill in Washington, D.C., where the Capitol building is situated. Called "the Hill" for short.

Casework: The errands that congressmen and their staffs perform for the people from their district or state. Examples of casework are when a congressman tracks down a voter's social security check, or arranges for emergency leave for someone in the armed forces.

Caucus/Conference: A meeting of all members of one party in one house of Congress. Democrats use the term caucus; Republicans prefer conference.

Checks and balances: The built-in structure of our federal government that distributes power so that no one branch or person can become too dominant.

Cloture: A vote to end debate; in the Senate, sixty senators must support the motion for cloture to be successful.

Coalition: A group of supporters that a candidate must assemble to help him win the election. A coalition might contribute money, endorsements, and workers to the campaign effort.

Coattail effect: The voting pattern that results when an overwhelmingly popular presidential candidate enables other members of his party, such as representatives and senators, to coast into office with him by hanging onto his "coattails."

Conference committee: A temporary panel consisting of representatives and senators who iron out differences in bills which have passed through each house of Congress. Once the conference committee forges the two versions into one, the bill goes back to each house for final approval, and then to the president.

Committee on Committees: A group of members set up by each party in each house to make committee assignments.

Congressional district: The area that a representative serves; usually shortened to "district."

Constituents: The people a representative or a senator serve; a representative's constituents are the people of his district, and a senator's constituents are the people of his state.

Crossover vote: Decision by a citizen to vote for candidate(s) of the other party. Thus, if a Republican party member votes for a Democratic candidate, that is an example of a crossover vote.

Democracy: A system of government in which the people rule, either directly or through representatives whom the people elect. The American government is a representative democracy.

Electoral college: The group of people who formally elect the President and Vice-President of our country. When we vote for candidates for these offices, we actually are voting for electors, who in turn cast their ballots for the candidate who wins a majority of votes in the state. Each state has a number of electors equal to its representation in Congress; thus, if a state has four Representatives and two Senators, it would have six electors—and six electoral votes. All of a state's electors are expected to cast their electoral votes for the candidate who received the most votes in their state.

Electors: Members of the electoral college.

Endorsement: A statement of support for a candidate. It can come from an individual, an organization, a newspaper, or a radio or television station.

Executive branch: The part of the federal government headed by the president. It includes a host of departments and agencies, all of which fall under the president's control.

Federalists: A political party in the early years of the nation that supported a powerful national government. Led by Alexander Hamilton, this group was wary of giving the people too much say in government, preferring to keep power in the hands of a select group of leaders.

Filibuster: An attempt by a senator or group of senators to block a bill by talking and talking, in the hope that the bill's supporters will withdraw it from consideration.

Floor: A term referring to a full meeting of the House and/or Senate. Thus, to discuss a bill on the floor is to discuss it before the entire membership.

Floor manager: A member of either house of Congress who is responsible for the handling of a bill on the chamber floor. A good floor manager must be an able politician who knows how to round up votes and how much he has to compromise in order to get his bill passed.

Folkway: An accepted, though unwritten, standard of behavior.

Franking privilege: The right of congressmen to send mail to their constituents at government expense. It can be a powerful weapon around election time.

Gerrymander: The political art of drawing the boundaries of a congressional district to suit the needs of one political party, at the expense of the other. Republican gerrymanders, thus, would yield the maximum possible number of congressional seats for its party, and as few as possible for the Democrats.

Hearing: A committee meeting at which witnesses give their opinions on a bill.

House of Representatives: One of the chambers of Congress. It consists of 435 members, who are apportioned to the 50 states on the basis of population.

Impeachment: The formal filing of charges against a public official. (This term does not mean the removal from office of the official; that can only happen after a trial is held to consider the impeachment.)

Incumbent: A candidate for office who already holds that office. Thus, a senator or representative running for reelection is an incumbent. The opponent is known as the challenger.

Independent: A voter or candidate not affiliated with a political party.

Joint committee: A committee consisting of members from both the House and the Senate.

Judicial branch: The branch of the federal government that judges legal disputes and interprets the United States Constitution.

Landslide: An election won by a wide margin.

Law: A binding rule that is enforced by the government.

Legislative branch: The lawmaking part of government. Congress is the legislative branch of the United States.

Lobbyist: A representative from an organization who tries to get various bills passed or defeated. For example, a lobbyist from an environmental group will try to influence Congress to make laws limiting pollution, and try to block laws that might increase pollution. The name comes from the place where these people used to try to talk to the legislators . . . in the lobby, right outside the chamber.

Logrolling: Trading votes on certain bills. To help each other out, two congressmen might agree to vote for each other's bills. An urban congressman, for instance, might go along with a bill to increase farm production, in return for the support of the "farm" congressman on a bill to give money to cities.

Majority leader (House): The floor leader of the majority party. His job is to help the party's policies get through the House.

Majority leader (Senate): The floor leader and top tactician of the majority party in the Senate. He, too, tries to guide the party's legislative goals through the chamber.

Majority party/Minority party: The majority party is the political party with the majority of seats in a given chamber of Congress, or Congress as a whole. The minority party is the political party with a lesser number of seats.

Markup: The committee's finishing touches on a bill; the time when the bill is pored over, line by line, before it is submitted to the floor.

Midterm election: Congressional elections held midway through a president's term of office. Thus, 1980 is a presidential election year, and 1982 will be a midterm election year.

Minority leader (House): Floor leader of the minority party of the House.

Minority leader (Senate): Floor leader of the minority party of the Senate.

Nominee: A candidate who wins his party's primary; the winner of the party's nomination for that office.

One-party district: A congressional district in which one party is clearly dominant—and always wins the elections.

Overriding a veto: Congress's way of overcoming a presidential veto of a bill by passing it by a two-thirds majority in both chambers.

Pigeonholing: A committee's method of blocking a bill by refusing to even consider it.

Platform: A national party's stands on important public issues.

Political party: An organization of voters, leaders, and officials on the local, state, and federal levels that tries to gain control of government through the nomination and election of its candidates. The two main political parties in the United States are the Republican party and the Democratic party.

Precinct: The smallest voting district. Each precinct has well-defined boundaries, and all the people living within them vote at the same polling place. There are some 150,000 precincts in the country.

President pro tempore of the Senate: The presiding officer of the Senate; he is elected by the majority party.

Primary election: An election held among members of a political party to determine the party's nominee for the regular election in November.

Quorum: The presence of more than half the members of the House or Senate, which is required to conduct official business. In the House, a quorum is 218 members; in the Senate, 51.

Reapportionment: The changing allotment of congressional districts to states, as dictated by the census taken every ten years. Under reapportionment, states that have gained substantially in population will pick up one or more districts, while those that have declined in population stand to lose one or more seats.

Recruit: A candidate for office who was sought out and encouraged to run by community and/or party leaders.

Redistricting: The redrawing of the boundaries of congressional districts. It is done every ten years, after the state knows, from reapportionment, how many districts it will have.

Report: The returning of a bill to the chamber floor by a committee. After a committee reports the bill to the House, the full membership then considers it on the floor.

Representative: A member of the United States House of Representatives. A representative also is sometimes called a congressman, congresswoman, or congressperson.

Select committee: A temporary committee established (usually by one house) to do a certain job. Once that job, which frequently involves an investigation of a person or agency in the executive branch, is finished, the committee disbands.

Self-starter: A candidate for office who decides on his own to run for office, without special encouragement from local leaders. He may get their support later, but he takes the first step by himself.

Senate: One of the two houses of Congress. It consists of two persons elected from each state, and one hundred members in all.

Senator: A member of the Senate. Senators also are congressmen, though, in practice, many people restrict the use of "congressman" to representatives.

Seniority: The length of service on a given House or Senate committee. Until recently, the member of the majority party of a committee automatically became the committee chairman. Because a member loses seniority when he changes committees, some congressmen are reluctant to do it.

Show horse: A member of Congress who tends to hunt for headlines to keep himself in the spotlight.

Speaker of the House: The presiding officer of the House of Representatives who is elected by a caucus of the majority party.

Standing committee: A permanent committee of Congress. The Senate has eighteen standing committees; the House has twenty-two. This is where bills are first considered, debated, and amended before going to the floor of either house.

Stump: The campaign trail. When a candidate goes on the stump, he is traveling around at a hectic pace, meeting and talking to voters. The phrase "taking the stump" means delivering a speech on the trail. It derives from the old method of campaigning on the frontier, when a candidate would get up on a tree stump to talk to the people.

Suffrage: The right to vote.

Two-party district: A congressional district in which the Republicans and Democrats both have a chance of winning the election. A two-party state exhibits the same sort of party balance.

Unicameral legislature: A lawmaking branch of government with only one chamber. Under the Articles of Confederation, Congress was a unicameral legislature.

Veto: The presidential power to block a bill by refusing to sign it. The bill then goes back to Congress, where the veto can be overridden if a two-thirds majority in each house votes in favor of the bill.

Whips: Party officers in each house of Congress who are the communication links between party leaders and party members. It is the job of the whips to round up support for party policies, and make sure its members are on hand for important votes.

Workhorse: A member of Congress who conscientiously does his work, even if it often may be tedious and unglamorous. A workhorse thoroughly applies himself to his legislative duties, while a show horse thoroughly applies himself to those duties which will get him attention in the media.

Bibliography

Barone, Michael; Ujifusa, Grant; and Matthews, Douglas. *The Almanac of American Politics 1980*. New York: Dutton, 1979. Everything you could ever want to know, from campaign expenditures to voting records, about your representatives, senators, and governors.

Bibby, John F., and Davidson, Roger H. *On Capitol Hill*. 2nd ed. Hinsdale, Ill.: Dryden, 1972. A study of campaigns for Congress and life on "the Hill" once there.

Bolling, Richard. *House Out of Order*. New York: Dutton, 1965. An argument for how the House should change its ways, written by a prominent representative from Missouri.

Clapp, Charles L. *The Congressman*. 2nd ed. Garden City, N.Y.: Anchor, 1964. A comprehensive collection of interviews and discussions with representatives on topics ranging from campaigns and committees to constituents.

Clark, Joseph S. *Congress—The Sapless Branch*. New York: Harper, 1965. A critique of Congress by the former senator from Pennsylvania.

Fenno, Richard F. *Congressmen in Committees*. Boston: Little, Brown, 1973. An analysis of the committee system.

Galloway, Dr. George B. *History of the United States House of Representatives*. 2nd ed. New York: Crowell, 1976. An informative chronicle of the first branch, from the Constitutional Convention to the present.

Hiebert, Ray E.; Jones, Robert F.; Lorenz, John d'Arc; Lotito, Ernest A., eds. *The Political Image Merchants: Strategies for the Seventies*. Washington, D.C.: Acropolis, 1975. Up-to-date collection of the latest in campaign techniques, by noted authorities in the field.

Leuthold, David A. *Electioneering in a Democracy*. New York: Wiley, 1968. A study of campaigns for the House, based on a detailed analysis of the 1962 elections in the San Francisco area.

Matthews, Donald R. *U.S. Senators and Their World*. Chapel Hill: University of North Carolina Press, 1960. A thorough treatment of all aspects of the Senate.

Price, H. Douglas. "The Electoral Arena." In *The Congress and America's Future*, 2nd ed., David B. Truman, ed. Englewood Cliffs, N.J.: Prentice-Hall, 1973. A study of changing voting trends in the twentieth century.

Ripley, Randall. *Congress—Process and Policy*. New York: Norton, 1975. A close look at how Congress functions.

Tacheron, Donald G., and Udall, Morris K. *The Job of the Congressman*.

144

Indianapolis: Bobbs-Merrill, 1966. A how-to analysis of the way our representatives do their work.

Weiss, Ann E. *The American Congress.* New York: Simon & Schuster, 1977. A simple, straightforward overview of Congress, especially good for young readers.

Wright, James. *You and Your Congressman.* 2nd ed. New York: Coward, McCann, 1972. An inside look at life in the House, and a representatives's connection with his constituents. Written by the representative from Texas.

Note: Extremely helpful studies of Congress are published by Congressional Quarterly, Inc., a Washington-based company. It puts out a variety of publications, all very valuable to students of Congress. Consult your librarian for details.

Index

DATE DUE
